MW00899351

Also by Terry Wilson:
Hiking the Real Estate Trail
Your study guide for the NC Real Estate Exam
(A nine CD Audio set)

Hiking the NC Real Estate Trail From Classroom to Trailhead

A Field Guide for the Newly Licensed Real Estate Agent

Terry Wilson SRES, GRI, CRS, DREI

To my wife, Deanna, first and always. Thanks to my family for their many talents and to my dear friend Len Elder, who has a nasty habit of pushing the right buttons and challenging me. Thanks also to Samantha Terres PLLC Attorney at Law for always getting back to me and always having the right answer, even when I don't want to hear it.

Table of Contents

Chapter 7: Putting one foot in front of the other OR what you must do regularly.   65

Chapter 8: Understanding the local fauna OR getting to know the people.   78

Chapter 9: Learning how to talk to the animals OR conflict resolution.   89

Foreword

In 1957 the North Carolina Real Estate Commission was created by the legislative body of our state. Its purpose was to oversee a new law that required those of us wanting to help others buy, sell, rent, lease or auction real property to have a real estate license. It was in that year that the real estate licensee was born in North Carolina.

Since that time, thousands of individuals have tried and failed at real estate while thousands more remain in the business. Starting and succeeding in real estate sales is very much like hiking the Appalachian Trail (AT). Many start on the trail but few finish. Is it because those that finish are smarter, stronger and more disciplined than those that fail? In part yes. But more importantly those that finish the trail prepare more effectively and understand what it takes to succeed. The same can be said for those that succeed in real estate. You must train every day and you must understand the trail maps and know your limits. This book will help you learn how to succeed in the practice of real estate and help you maintain your focus. Finally, it will help you pace yourself and assist you in learning your maps so you can find your way down these many real estate trails.

I wrote this book because I have a passion for helping real estate agents succeed. I don't know where it comes from but I find great joy when an agent calls to tell me about their first closing or how exciting it was to push their first For Sale sign into a client's yard. I hope to hear from you. I hope you'll share the joy of your first listing. I still remember mine. I remember pushing the sign into this hard Carolina clay and realizing I should pack a sledge hammer in my trunk for future listings.

I look back on the years that I have been in real estate. I have now been a real estate agent longer than I was an IBM employee – a thought I would never have dreamed of so many years ago. In fact, I entered this business more as an afterthought than a well thought out life plan; but I am here to stay. I hope the same can be said for you no matter how you came to acquire your license.

I want you to know that in many ways this is one of the most generous arenas you will ever enter. Even as each agent is their own company and we are all competitors, I so admire how generous the vast majority of agents are to share their time, tips and tricks with other agents – even other companies' agents – to help them grow their business. I hope that as you grow you will also give back and share your advice and counsel to new and newer agents.

As a real estate instructor I make annual treks to the REEA (Real Estate Educators Association) conference. I have the great pleasure of meeting with hundreds of instructors from across the country. I hear their stories (good and bad) and we share classroom tips and tricks (also good and bad). They are an incredibly generous group. I mention this here because we also talk about the status of real estate in each of our states. Sure North Carolina has struggled, as has the rest of the country, but I must say you have chosen the right state in which to practice real estate. Our market is healing and will continue to grow for a long, long time. And although I believe this to be true, you are about to embark on a journey with many peaks and valleys, with views beyond your imagination and wild animals to confront. Do not enter this chosen career blindly. Do not "wing it" and do not look at your career as anything less than the most professional of career choices. As with every true professional, stay on top of your education and your market.

One final thought before we begin our hike, there are many things we discuss at the REEA conventions but one that regularly pops up during breaks and in private conversations is our thoughts and experiences with each of our state's Real Estate Commissions. As I've mentioned, the North Carolina Real Estate Commission was created in 1957 primarily to protect those buying and selling real estate. But they are also here to serve you and aid you on your journey. And in my opinion, they have the finest and most dedicated staff of them all. From the departments of education to licensing to legal, take advantage of their offerings. They want you to call them. They want to help you find the answers to your questions and guide you when the trail becomes confusing. Believe me when I say how blessed we are to have this commission as our guiding light.

Preface

You've passed your real estate state exam, joined the local Realtor® organization and now you're raring to go... But to where, how do you get started, what do you do first?

This book will help you get your business up and running with clear guidance on what you need to do before you set off down the trail and the steps you need to take early in your hike. It will help you stay focused using goal setting and planning tips and help you understand how to develop your buyer and seller client base so you can close more transactions. It will assist you in learning the call of the wild" and how to communicate with the various animals you meet along the way. And it provides guidance to help you complete this long journey where many before you have failed.

In essence, it is a hiking guide. A guide that will assist you in deciding which firm to join, how to get started in the business, what to do in the first few weeks after you receive your license and advice to help you grow your business.

Just as with all hiking guides this book is meant to be marked up, scribbled on, copied and consulted regularly during your real estate hike. Throughout the book there are lined areas and several blank pages in the back for your notes, drawings, ah-ha moments and general musings.

It follows the structure of guide books; with the early chapters helping you to prepare for your hike and the later chapters showing you the various flora and fauna you will meet along your journey, the various trails you can take and what you should do each and every day to grow your business and become a better hiker.

Occasionally you will see the Appalachian Trail symbol. These indicate comments I feel warrant special attention. They are the caution signs throughout your journey. And at the end of each chapter is a Trail Log, so you can write notes that reflect on your journey as you walk this trail.

The Appendices contain checklists and information I welcome you to copy and/or use in your business.

I wish you the greatest of luck as you venture onto this great trail called real estate. If you have a question, comment or suggestions please feel free to contact me at:
Terry@wilsonrealtync.com.

Thank you purchasing this book; I hope you enjoy reading it as much as I did writing it and I hope its prose benefit you during your hike in these woods we call real estate.

Chapter 1: Why hike the trail?

Of all the questions raised when starting a real estate career, this one is probably the most important. Do you really know why you want to help others buy and sell real estate? Before going deeper into this guide, check out Appendix A and review the BIG WHY exercise.

The BIG WHY is what motivates everyone. Professional football players are driven to hurl themselves around the field taking incredible health risks for one BIG WHY – The Super bowl ring. Appalachian Trail (AT) thru-hikers get up every day and hike the 2,175 mile trail in sometimes horrid conditions for one BIG WHY – to experience this: The Northern Terminus at Mt. Katahdin…

Also consider that we live on a small rock that spins on its axis at approximately 1,038 miles per hour; I say approximately because it very much depends on where you are standing at the moment. As it spins, our little top hurls itself around a distant sun at 67,000 miles per hour – a speed that would allow you to leave Raleigh NC at 11:57AM and arrive in Los Angeles CA less than three minutes later, just in time for your noon lunch. Assuming you would still want lunch. Everything you do, you say and you accomplish, everyone you meet, help, hate and love will all exist in one lifetime on this tiny rock spinning around a relatively small sun at a speed that is amazingly difficult to fathom. I can't think of a better reason than this to understand your BIG WHY when it comes to joining the ranks of Realtors.

Helping others buy and sell real estate can be incredibly rewarding and financially lucrative. But it also has as many frustrations and setbacks as the AT. You may already know the BIG WHY. But if you aren't sure what your BIG WHY is, take a few minutes and check out Appendix A.

Without knowing your BIG WHY it is easy to lose focus and wonder why you're dealing with the daily slings and arrows. In other words, it's hard to get up every day and fight the good fight if you don't know what you're fighting for.

And please don't say it is for the money. There are many ways (many of them easier than real estate) to make money. What do you want to do with that money? What purpose does it serve? I occasionally hear this answer in pre-licensing classes when I ask students why they are taking the class. It is not uncommon for those students to perform poorly or simply drop out of the class when the going gets tough. Money for its own sake is not a strong enough motivator to struggle through the many slings and arrows you will face in this business. Many studies have shown that poor people are, in general, happier than affluent people. If it were truly about the money this should not be true. Sure, having money is nice and even necessary but in the end it will not be the sole motivator that sustains you in this business.

Once you know your BIG WHY, make it your laptop's screen saver, and write it on sticky notes all over your house. Put it in your car, your purse, your wallet and your spouse's purse or wallet. In other words constantly remind yourself what you are trying to accomplish and why.

Consider this, on July 31st 2011 Jennifer Pharr Davis, 28, completed the fastest hike of the 2,175 mile Appalachian Trail, averaging 46.9 miles per day. She trimmed 26 hours off of the previous record. When asked why she did it, this was her quote:

"I consider it to be a love story. I love the trail and far more than that I love my husband. Beyond romance, I believe true love is best demonstrated through endurance and perseverance. That is what got me through the bad weather, intense pain and many hardships this summer –

a devotion to the trail and a complete trust and shared intimacy with my husband."

Now that's a BIG WHY! If you want to read more about Jennifer's story, visit: www.jenniferpharrdavis.tumblr.com

Now you hopefully know your BIG WHY and regardless of the reason, only you know why you got your real estate license and why you've chosen a career as a real estate agent ready to assist others with buying and selling real property. Whatever your reason, you're at the trail head ready to go. But wait are you prepared? Before setting off on the trail that lies ahead, let's talk about...

Planning your hike

It is fair to say that you would never drive to the AT's southern trail head, located at Springer Mountain in Georgia, and start a thru-hike (one that goes the entire length of the AT). No, planning your hike is just as crucial as being in good enough shape to hike it.

Hundreds of average Joes and Janes have succeeded in hiking the AT. Thousands of others have started and failed, some within a few days and some within a few weeks. If these folks can do it, what makes them different? Why can they complete a thru-hike when they have nothing special? In my opinion, two words... preparation and drive.

Many a real estate agent has had the drive but lacked preparation. They ran scattered and full force working 10, 12, sometimes 15 hours per day; that is until those initial leads dried up and there they stood with no idea where to go. Quite literally for many of them it was the equivalent of running into the Appalachian Trail full of enthusiasm and excitement until becoming exhausted and disoriented with no idea where they were or where they were headed.

Your drive comes from your BIG WHY. Preparation is what keeps you from simply using all that initial adrenalin and excitement in the wrong way. Preparing for your career will save you hours of wasted time and help you maintain balance between your work life and personal life. We all have a different situation. Some are married or in a relationship, some are single, some are single parents and some are married with several children. There is school, sports, band, ballet, plays, church and the list goes on and on. Is there a one-size-fits-all approach to preparation? Thankfully there is. How it is implemented may vary but we all must check these items off our list. The most important item has been taken care of and you can check it off… you got your license. Congratulations. Now what?

Trail Log:

_____

_____

_____

_____

_____

_____

_____

_____

_____

_____

_____

_____

_____

_____

_____

_____

_____

_____

_____

_____

_____

Chapter 2: Trail orientation OR your education requirements.

As a brand new North Carolina licensee your status is most likely Provisional Broker. You must remove this status within three years from the date you got your license. To do so you must take at least one post-licensing course each year from the date you received your license (i.e. by the first, second and third anniversary of the date of your license)

Please do yourself a favor and put this on your calendar now. I teach post-licensing courses and I can't tell you how many times an agent has come into the class completely stressed out because their license will be set to inactive status two days from the end of the class and if they don't pass the class (yes, there is an exam) then they will not be allowed to sell real estate. Try telling that to the five buyers and seven sellers you are currently working with. To pour a little salt in the wound, those five buyer and seven seller clients actually belong to your real estate firm which means should you become inactive, they may very well be assigned to another agent as an orphaned account. Ouch! Or worse, that one particular buyer you've been working with for months has to buy now and they cannot wait for you to reactivate your license so they turn to another agent who is more than happy to assist them. You might get a referral fee, but more than likely you will not, and either way it's a lot less than the commission you would have earned had you been diligent in taking your post licensing courses.

Can you do all three post-licensing courses in the first year? Yes you can. Should you? Well that depends, they do cost money, can you afford it? They do take time (30 hours for each), can you afford the time? I believe you can afford the time more than you will once your business takes off. I personally believe you should take all three courses in your first year and remove your Provisional Broker status. Ask yourself, do you really want to be in a 30 hour class in your third year from the date you got your license while trying to juggle all the buyers and sellers you have cultivated over the last three years along with the numerous closings you have scheduled (one of which falls on the same day as class... And yes,

Real Estate Commission rules require that you attend closing on behalf of your client!)? Not to mention the stress of trying to get that last class in before the third anniversary of your license.

I think there is another very important reason to complete all three courses in your first year. Ask yourself honestly how much information you really retained from pre-licensing. If you're like most students, you purged that information the moment you walked out of the state exam. It's nobody's fault, we simply feel we no longer need the information so we do a good old fashioned system dump. The only problem is that much of what you learn in pre-licensing is important to your real estate career. The post-licensing courses will help you retain that information for the long term.

Two other quick notes regarding education: First, the post-licensing courses can be taken in any order which will make scheduling them a little easier. Second, post-licensing courses do NOT count toward your Continuing Education which you will need to complete between the next July 1st after you received your license and June 10th of the following year. (See Appendix C for more information on education)

I think one of the biggest mistakes agents make (regardless of the number of years they've been in the business) is waiting until the last minute to complete their Continuing Education. As a professional, why wouldn't you want to be the first to know the changes that could and often do directly affect your clients? As a hiker would you rather know the trail has been changed to a dead end BEFORE you walk its length or after?

⋔ If you want to be a professional with longevity, get your education in early rather than late. Be the leader on changes not the follower. Imagine walking into a listing presentation with a potential seller armed with the knowledge of upcoming contract changes and being able to explain to the seller how it will affect them and what they need to know while the competing agents

6

are still working from outdated information. I'd be impressed, wouldn't you?

Becoming a trail master OR a thought on furthering your education

There are dozens if not hundreds of real estate designations available with more, it seems, being offered every day. Look at the letters next to my name – GRI, CRS, SRES, DREI. I doubt you gave them a second thought when you picked up this book and I doubt they were the reason you decided to read it. If they did influence you, congratulations you are in the 1% club (read on). In my opinion buyers and sellers could not give a hoot about them either since, in general, they hire real estate agents for the following reasons: 1. They like the agent. 2. They trust the agent. 3. They believe the agent has their best interests in mind. 4. They believe the agent has market knowledge.

If you were a seller or a buyer and the agent you were interviewing met the four criteria I describe above, would you care that much about the designations they hold? Would it really make that big of a difference? Several years ago a national firm conducted a study and discovered that 1% of buyers and sellers cared about designations. 1%!! That is a very small pool of potential clients and with the cost to obtain many of these designations the return on your educational expenses is correspondingly small.

As noted I have several designations. Were they worth it? I've never had a seller or buyer ask about them; even though they are right next to my name. And I've never, knowingly, been hired as a direct result of them. There is one designation, Distinguished Real Estate Instructor (DREI), which I cherish more than any of the others. It was a very tough and arduous trail but the view (i.e. the education) was worth it.

🄰 Do yourself and your pocket-book a favor. If the designation comes with the education go for it, but don't pursue the education for the sake of the designation. Knowing your BIG WHY will help you determine what, if any, additional education you may need.

7

Trail Log:

Chapter 3: Selecting your hiking buddies OR which firm should you affiliate with?

Which trail head do I start on OR picking your firm

Many new agents believe this is a critical first step that has life changing consequences. Relax, this step is not as dramatic, traumatic or whatever other "ic" you may think of. First let's dispel a myth.

Myth: the firm is interested in me, I must be special.
The truth: You are special but for the most part if you have a license and you have a heart beat and you show an inkling of motivation and drive, most firms will bring you aboard. There are a few firms that run you through personality tests to see if you're a good fit and I say, *"Good for them."* I don't question (nor do I have a right to) their hiring methodologies. But in general if you have a license, you're reasonably well groomed, you don't smell odd and you're mildly motivated… you're hired!

Why is it important to understand this? Because just as you would interview a trail guide to make sure they are a good fit for you, your interview with the firm is not about them interviewing you, it's about you interviewing them. Please understand that if you are successful, then so too is the firm. After all, they will take a percentage of every commission you earn. The more money you make, the more money they make.

When interviewing firms, keep in mind the questions that you want to ask to help you get up and running and have a successful career (see Appendix D for a detailed list of questions). In general you want to make sure the firm fits your needs in the following ways…

You will rely on and need the knowledge of your Broker-in-Charge (BIC) during your first few months more than you will over the next several years because once you have done a listing presentation one or two times you start to get a feel for it. Once you've completed your second or third Offer to Purchase and Contract you start to understand how it works; the same is true with settlement meetings (commonly referred to as Closing). In the beginning though, those contracts and transaction processes are as big as the AT mountains you see on the horizon. So, how available is the BIC. After all if they are responsible for dozens if not hundreds of agents, will they have time for you?

⬆ Note many firms have other resources and personnel to assist you should you need help so don't rule out a large firm with many agents supervised by one BIC, just be sure there are resources there when you need them.

What education opportunities do they have? Many firms have their own in-house education and it is often mandatory. Is it broken up to allow you to apply what you've learned – as if you've sipped from a babbling brook – or is it intense training that will leave you feeling like you drank from a raging waterfall? Don't dismiss small firms in this area. They may not have formal training programs in traditional classroom environments but if they are meeting with you one-on-one to role play and walk you through the real estate transaction process that can be even more beneficial than a traditional classroom environment.

Education can be a tricky thing because you feel very productive when you've attended the Tuesday sales meeting and listened to experienced agents ideas. You've logged on to the firm's website and watched the one hour instructional video on Closing Techniques. You've read the latest Realtor magazine, studied the inventory of your local MLS, joined in a caravan to see your company's listings and caught up with the latest real estate trends on Inman.com... Good for you, it looks like you had a productive day. But did you? How many people did you actually talk to that were in the market to buy and/or sell a home. It's like knowing the AT like the back of your hand by studying every map, reading every successful hiker's journal and researching the latest in backpacking equipment but never actually hiking the trail yourself.

Sure education is important but it should never be placed in front of seeking out clients and customers to work with. All that knowledge will do you no good if you don't have anybody to use it on. Believe me, when I started in this business I wanted to know every aspect of the business before I talked with my first seller or buyer. I'll let you in on a secret, you will never know enough about this business to be ready for every buyer or seller in every situation. They say real estate is local. So too are the problems and experiences you will have. Every real estate transaction is different and you will *always* learn something new with each one of them.

 The education your brokerage firm provides is important, but in my opinion, it should never be placed above seeking out buyers and/or sellers.

You will learn as you go. You will face new and exciting (and by exciting, I mean scary) challenges in almost every transaction. This is why it is important that you have a reliable source (whether it is the BIC, the office staff or experienced brokers) to rely on to help you quickly find answers. If you do not feel that is the case during the interview process, it will most likely not be the case when you need it the most.

Is it critical the firm have lots of listings, robust websites, tens if not hundreds of agents, a national presence? Yes and no. I will say that at one time large firms had many advantages over small firms. However, the internet and all its offerings have changed that. Let me ask you something, if you were in the market to purchase a home today, where would you start? On the internet, most likely, and where on the internet would you go? Well as of 2011, you would probably go to Zillow.com or Trulia.com or maybe Realtor.com. The point is if your MLS shares its listings with these sites (and most do) then does it really matter whether you're a national firm putting that listing on Zillow.com or a local one? The internet has now made it so even small firms can provide the same exposure of their listing inventory as large firms do. And with the convenience of Virtual Assistants, low cost websites, inexpensive toll-free numbers, and the reduced need for expensive office space, small firms can appear to the consuming public as big as the largest firms.

Some sellers still believe that large firms offer them greater opportunities to sell their home. Does it? I don't think so, but if the seller believes it you have to consider that. However, I do believe sellers are quickly realizing that size doesn't matter as much as it once did, and what does matter is the service provided by their agent and the costs associated with the sale of their home.

So should you go small, medium or large? Only you can answer that based on your impressions of the various firms you interview, their answers to the questions you ask, and the feeling you have about that firm, its agents and its BIC.

Regardless of the size of the firm you choose, finding the right firm for you has never been easier because you no longer have to choose between local exposure, regional exposure, and national exposure. The internet and all its trappings have, in my opinion, leveled the playing field.

Further, there is no perfect firm. None of them will hold your hand every step of the way. It simply is a matter of the time they have available to devote to you, especially if the BIC is a competing BIC (one who also lists and sells property). It is critical to remember you have chosen to hike this trail, and you will hike it alone regardless of which firm you choose. Sure there will be plenty of support along the way but in the end, we all hike this trail alone. Your education is up to you... seek it out and pursue it. If you wait for your BIC to tell you what to do next, you may be waiting a long time. Sorry, I mean a short time because you won't be in the business long. It is your business – you need to treat as such.

How many firms should you interview? I suggest at least one from each of the above categories. But what if you decide on one and you discover it wasn't everything you thought it would be? Here's something that should give you peace of mind... switching firms because the one you initially chose did not work out is not the stigma you may think it is. Remember, there are four reasons buyers and sellers hire you:

1. They like you.
2. They trust you.

3. They believe you have their best interests in mind.
4. They believe you have good market knowledge.

The first three are more important than the last. Let's face it, if you don't like someone or you don't trust them or you don't believe they have your best interests in mind do you really care how much they know?

Funny thing is there is no mention of the firm because people hire YOU. Oh I suppose if you were with the firm "We Scam 'Em Realty" they may think twice about hiring you, but in general you are the firm and you are who they hire.

As part of your interview process you must understand the firm's policies regarding taking listings and buyer clients with you should you decide to leave the firm. Remember that the listing belongs to the firm and so too does the buyer client. You have no unilateral right to take them with you should you leave the firm nor do you have a right to indicate or imply to your clients that they can exit the listing or buyer agency agreement and move with you to a new firm. Thoroughly review any prospective firm's policies so you understand the consequences should you change firms.

Some firms allow you to take the clients with you, some don't. Some allow you to receive a commission on a client that was under contract while you were with the firm but at a reduced commission split. Others will not allow you to be paid at all while still others let you keep your commission as if you had never left.

 Know all of the firm's policies before you decide to join that firm.

The best campsites OR the various types of firms
Regardless of whether you choose a national firm or a local mom and pop shop, there are many types of firms to choose from. You may decide to sit in a model home for a builder or work only with buyers at a buyer-

agency firm. You might like to work with a limited services firm or take the traditional general-brokerage trail and join a full-service firm. Let's take a look at each…

Builders

If you decide to join a builder you may be able to sit in a nicely decorated model home and let the buyers come to you. Of course because you work for the builder you will not be able to pursue these buyers should they decide to buy elsewhere. However, this approach can be lucrative. It can also be very lonely, dangerous and unsuccessful should you be placed in a model home in a slow moving neighborhood or with a builder of poor quality. If you decide to join a builder, do your homework. Ask them to show how many homes they've sold and the average days-on-market for those homes. What neighborhood will you be assigned to? Is that neighborhood convenient for you? Does it look safe? Is it a lively neighborhood or one that is mostly empty lots and half built homes? What is your personal life like, many builders require you to work weekends, which makes perfect sense since this is when the buyers are out and about the most. You may get two days off during the week but they may not be together, or you may be required to work six days a week. Can your personal life accommodate this type of schedule?

The advantage of working with a builder is that the buyers will come to you. But that is only true if you pick the right builder in the right neighborhood. You may have to prove your worth before the builder gives you a cherry-picked neighborhood, but be sure the builder can offer that should you meet their criterion.

Limited brokerage firms

Limited brokerage firms assist sellers in the listing of their homes but limit the service they offer the seller. Some have a menu of services that range from charging the seller an upfront fee for placing the listing in the local MLS and then washing their hands of any further service to a complete service listing in which the firm provides all listing service needs.

In my opinion, sellers (just as we all are) are willing to pay full price for quality service. These firms tend to rise and fall and they simply have not taken root as a preferred provider of service. On the surface they offer a compelling business model – for a set fee they may place the seller's home in the local MLS, place a sign and lockbox on the property and provide a brochure box (possibly with a starter supply of brochures) and maybe an advertisement in a local real estate magazine. In addition they will offer the listing on their website and other websites that the local MLS feeds. However, that is often where their service stops. The seller is left to their own devices regarding showing the home and negotiating and understanding contracts.

I believe these firms have not gained more ground than they have because once a seller discovers the difficulty of working the transaction and coordinating the showings without the aid of a real estate agent, they realize they may not have gotten their money's worth. Further, if other firms show the home and their buyer client is interested in making an offer, that firm will be dealing directly with the seller. Of course the seller is not their client but they may be looking for advice and counsel which can create an awkward situation and requires careful attention by the agent to protect her client's interests while tending to the fiduciary duties she also owes her buyer client.

Should you choose to work for a Limited Brokerage firm, remember your fiduciary duties; they are not dismissed simply because the firm only offers to place a sign in the yard and put the listing in the local MLS. As that seller's agent, the firm's (and your) fiduciary duties are no less than a full service firm who is with the client from listing to closing. How will you assure you are fulfilling those duties in a limited service environment? You need to be sure you have an adequate answer to this question should you decide to join a limited service firm.

Full service firms
Just as the name implies these are firms that are with the client from beginning to end. The firm (AKA agent) provides all the services necessary to assist their client in selling, purchasing and closing on their

home. The vast majority of firms are full service firms with good reason because, in my opinion, buyers and sellers will always be willing to pay for quality service to assure they are well protected and all the i's are dotted and t's are crossed.

VOWs (Virtual Office Websites)

Although these are rare, I suspect they will continue to grow as we become a more interconnected and "interneted" world. In essence their office is in the virtual world of the internet. They have no true physical office. The clients are vetted and created on their website. Leads are generated from the website and provided to the agents (see Lead Generation Firms).

I do not think VOWs are a viable option for new agents for many reasons. Where will your BIC be? How will they directly and actively supervise you? What support will you get during a transaction? Does the VOW properly follow NC Real Estate Commission rules regarding agency disclosure? Not an easy task when you are not sitting across the table from the consumer while you present the Working with Real Estate Agents Brochure. Is the VOWs website generating enough viable leads? Just to name a few of my concerns.

Lead generation firms

Although most, if not all, firms will generate leads (if they don't, they probably won't be in business long), some firms specialize in lead generation for their agents. Leads are the carrot at the end of the stick these firms offer new recruits. Many of these leads are generated from the company's website. Think back to the last website that asked you to register before obtaining your requested information. Were you truthful in all your answers – maybe, but maybe not? Many of these leads are wild goose chases and these firms may require you to chase them all (or at least a sizable number of them) or your future leads may be limited in quality and quantity. Are you prepared to dial-for-dollars? Before agreeing to join a firm like this, ask yourself if you would prefer to chase one hundred unknown, unsourced and unverified leads or one lead provided to you by your friends and family? Do not be lured by the number of leads promised you. Remember there is no easy trail on the AT that leads to the Northern Terminus. Do your homework and be careful about the statistical claims made by these companies. As Mark Twain is oft quoted, *"There are lies, damn lies and statistics."* Wise words indeed...

It may sound like I am completely against lead generation firms or VOWs. I am not, but I am cautious of the many claims I have heard them make and the disappointment agents have experienced after trying and failing at these firms.

Referral firms
Although these are usually firms within other firms; hanging your real estate license with a referral company is a viable option if you are not able to work the business full time or even part time. As a member of the referral firm, you may not hold yourself out as being available to help others buy or sell real estate but because you are on active status and under the care of a BIC, you can collect a referral fee. These firms are usually lower in cost to join and you may not have to pay the local MLS or Realtor dues. If you have contacts interested in buying and selling real estate but you simply cannot afford the time or money to devote yourself to real estate, consider affiliating your license with a referral company.

 If you decide to join a referral firm, you must maintain an active license to receive a referral fee. To keep your license active you will have to pay the annual NC RE Commission fee and complete your Continuing Education each year; plus you must complete all three 30 hour post-license courses. Never neglect your education.

Company fee structures
Many firms, if not most firms, charge a fee. They may call it a monthly desk fee, or admin fee, or simply a fee. It is a cost above and beyond your MLS fees, Realtor dues, the NC RE Commission's annual fee, and other fees required by various public and private entities. In the past

these fees ranged anywhere from tens of dollars to thousands of dollars per month. (Several years ago I left a national firm after they decided to increase their fee to one thousand two hundred dollars per month. Admittedly, I kept 100% of my commission, but if I didn't have a closing I still owed that fee.) However, they usually corresponded with the commission split structure. As such, the lower the fee the less commission you earned and vice versa.

As business models have evolved to keep up with the ever changing world of real estate, so too have fee structures. There are now firms that offer transaction based fees (i.e. a fee you pay only when you have a closing) in addition to monthly desk fees, but for this you receive a higher commission split. Then there are firms that charge a flat fee each month but the commission split varies based on your production. Yet there are other firms that charge small fees, but they take a greater amount of your commission. And finally there are those that do not charge a fee and still provide a generous commission split to the agent. The old saying, *"there is no such thing as a free lunch"* is alive and well. In general you will pay the firm in fees or in commission splits.

 Fees should correspond to the amount of support and education a firm offers. If a firm charges a high desk fee and/or a lower commission split you should expect, in return, quality education, a back office and other advantages to make your business life easier and more productive.

Although I cannot discuss the merits of these fee structure plans because their advantages and disadvantages depend entirely upon your personal circumstances, be sure you discuss with each firm their fee structure and commission split and weigh that against your personal financial situation and financial goals.

Do I hike straight through or take time off (full VS part time)

This is a tough question to answer because everyone's situation is different. I can only offer my view on what I have done and what I have seen other agents do and share with you our successes and failures.

Although I had my license and I had been investing in real estate for several years, I started helping others buy and sell real estate in 1997. I truly enjoyed the benefits of a strong national real estate market and an even stronger local market in the burgeoning city of Charlotte, NC. Did I work hard? You bet. Remember you work in poor markets and healthy markets because a poor market has fewer opportunities but it also has fewer agents to compete with; whereas a healthy market has many opportunities, but many more agents. Put another way, the more deer there are the more hunters there are to compete for them.

Once I decided to help others buy and sell real estate, I chose to dive in full time. Primarily because I had had enough of Corporate America and I just couldn't see myself sitting behind a desk 10 hours a day for another 20 years. Ironically that was my paradigm so that's what I did the first few months I was in the business until I realized that there would be no paycheck at the end of the week unless I got off my butt and went out there and got it. Don't make the same mistake. But I digress…

If you can afford to dive in full time, you should do it. However, you need to have a minimum of 6 - 8 months living expenses in the bank or another source of income to support you until your business is up and running.

 This does not include your retirement accounts. Unless you have no choice, and I hope you do, please do not touch these accounts to start a real estate career.

You may have your first closing in the first three weeks; you may go three months or longer before you see your first closing. Unless you know someone that is interested in buying the moment you join a firm and they have cash, and you've found them the perfect home, I would plan on three to six months not three to six weeks.

I'm not trying to be a naysayer but the reality is and the odds are that given both the real estate and lending environments we are in and will be in for the foreseeable future, it will take longer not shorter to close your first transaction. To wit, several firms have changed the names of their new agent courses to better reflect the length of time a new agent can realistically experience their first listing and/or first closing. Gone are creative course titles like, "Three Listings, Two Closings in Four Months" and similarly sounding names.

Should you interview a firm that promises success within the first few weeks or a specific number of transactions or closings in a specific time frame, ask them to prove it. Ask to interview several agents that have worked the company's system; does the claim hold true?

If you have your first closing within your first three weeks congratulations! Although this is cause for celebration, it is only one closing and it may not carry you very far without another one right around the corner. Be frugal and smart about starting your business. Have adequate savings or another source of income.

Part time:
Ok, so you don't have enough savings or you don't want to spend them but you want to get started in real estate anyway. Well then you have to be willing to agree to the following (initial next to each statement you agree to commit to:

_____ I am willing to work to grow my real estate business during my off work hours even if I have had a difficult or exhausting day.

_____ I am willing to contact a minimum number of potential buyers and sellers, friends and/or family members either in person or by phone even if I have had an exhausting or difficult day.

_____ I am willing to work weekends and/or other days off to either prospect for buyers and/or sellers or show properties to potential buyers.

_____ If necessary, I am willing to take a day of vacation to attend a closing or a required real estate class because I recognize it is a NC Real Estate Commission requirement.

Ok, so the above commitments may seem rather harsh but do recognize that if you don't make real estate a priority it will always sit on the back burner and eventually cool to the point where the fire has died. If I've seen it once, I've seen it a hundred times.

You may not be able to work on real estate full time but is it what you ultimately want? Are you willing to suffer some short term pain to grow your real estate career while transitioning from your other job? This is why the BIG WHY is so important. You have to know what you're fighting for. I'm often asked as a real estate instructor and broker owner of a small but growing firm how many hours of the day I work. The problem is I don't look at it as work because I love what I do so whether it is two hours or 20 I'm happy.

Working real estate part time is not a sustainable long term career choice. Should you decide to work in real estate part time but you would like to grow your business, it is imperative that you have a plan to transition to full time at some point. To paraphrase the Bible, we cannot serve two masters; this advice is as true today as when it was written.

Trail Log:

Chapter 4: Limbering up for your hike OR your first few weeks in real estate.

I'm going to assume that you have chosen a full time career in real estate. If you're part time, you will need to perform these same steps but you may need more than a week.

In spite of what you may think, your first week will not make or break you. In fact if you've wisely set money aside, your first month or six will not make or break you. However, it is important to start off on the right foot. Appendix B has a checklist of things for you to perform in your first week but I would like to spend a few minutes sharing with you what to expect.

As a full time agent, you must answer this question. **Are you a self starter? (Yes or no)** _____ This is an important question you must answer honestly because if you've chosen a firm that has a small office or no office (Provisional Brokers be sure you are being directly and actively supervised by your BIC) then you may spend much of your day working from home. Of course, even large firms afford you this opportunity. So are you a self starter? If you are like me, I find that I need to shower, shave, and get dressed so I can go into the office (even if that office is just down the hall from my bedroom). Otherwise, I find myself doing household chores; a necessary activity, and one that brings a sense of satisfaction, but not one that will effectively help me grow my business.

Be cautious when working from your home. It is easy to end the day feeling a great sense of accomplishment because of all the chores that were completed but, again, how much of your time was spent developing your business. Never be satisfied if your day ends with little to no business development activity; no matter how much you accomplished.

↑ Never under-estimate the power of dressing for success even if it's in your own home.

In general your first couple of days will be spent getting oriented with your new firm - their policies and procedures, meeting the office staff and generally getting a lay of the land. Basically you're meeting your hiking buddies and laying out your hiking strategy.

You need to do this. However, here are the top three things you must try to accomplish in your first week at your new firm.

1. Get on the MLS (you may have to sign up for a class but get it scheduled ASAP). Why? The MLS is essentially your trail map; it contains all the products that are available for you to sell; or all the trails available to hike.

2. Develop a list of the names, addresses, email and phone number of people you know or you know of; do not leave anyone out (even if you don't like them). This is your circle of influence. This is the group that is going to help you launch your career. You thought you were a one person show? Nope! These people will be your greatest sales force because they know you, they like you, they respect you and they believe you have theirs and other peoples best interests at heart. But the most important thing is that the vast majority of them want to help you succeed.

A few thoughts about asking for help. Maybe it is because we feel independent that we chose to hike this real estate trail alone but that independence also hampers us from asking for help when we need it the most. I promise you your friends and family want to help you succeed. But don't assume they are going to go out of their way without a little prompting.

Think of it this way, you see a hiker standing on the side of the trail. You may ask if they need help but more than likely you'll assume they are resting or enjoying the view so off you go, but if they ask you for water,

24

you will unquestionably provide it. The same is true for your friends and family. Ask them for water. Ask them for help, they will provide it. Remember though, they have busy lives too so you may not presume that if you've asked them for help once and they failed to deliver that they are not interested in helping you; it simply may be a matter of memory. Be sure to regularly remind them and reeducate them on what you do and how they can help.

Many years ago a co-worker told me, *"You have to teach people how you want to be treated."* I've never forgotten those words and the same can be said for re-educating people on what you do. Everyone plays a role in life and if you've just received your license and you're embarking on a career in real estate, I can assure you that real estate agent is not the first role your friends and family think you play; should you doubt me, ask a couple of your friends and family members what they think of when describing you. You will have to spend time re-educating them and teaching them your new role so they see you in a new light.

The best way to build your business is with past clients and referrals but you can't get there until you actually have those past clients. Your friend's and family's referrals will help you establish your business and give you a receptive audience while you're still learning the ropes and making mistakes – trust me, you'll make mistakes (unless, of course, you prefer to call them something else).

As indicated above, I've asked you to put a list of names together. So what are you going to do with this list? You will use it to regularly contact and remind these folks you're in the business of assisting others with buying and selling real estate.

3. Develop your 10 second elevator speech. Here's the funny thing about this business, it hasn't changed in 50 years and probably never will change. Oh sure the methods of communication will change, contracts will change, homes will change but the bottom line is this is a people business. We really don't sell homes as much as we sell relationships.

Having a 10 second elevator speech gives you the opportunity to clearly lay out what you do, why you do it, who you can help, how you can help them and why you can help them

If you were stuck in an elevator with someone and they asked you what you do and you said, *"I'm a Realtor."* you've just lumped yourself in with tens of thousands of other licensees and, in all likelihood, established the grounds for a nice quiet elevator ride. However, if you were to say something like:

"I assist sellers whose homes are potentially worth less than the amount they owe and are therefore potential short sales. Helping individuals get out of financial crisis is the primary reason I entered real estate. My banking background assures that I know the right questions to ask the sellers and with the many contacts I have at various banks, I can provide the right information to the right parties assuring we get a quick decision of the bank's acceptance."

they might just remember you. In fact you may have prompted the person you're talking with to specifically think of someone they know who needs your services. In essence, instead of telling them to think about the color purple, you told them to think about a purple Grizzly bear wearing a pair of Groucho Marx glasses and juggling her cubs while standing on her hind two feet in a field of sunflowers wearing a Mickey Mouse hat (try to get that image out of your head). The more specific you can be the more they can help you. As Tom Cruise said in the movie Jerry Maguire, *"Help me help you."* Then again, if you don't receive a lead from the person you just shared your elevator speech with, the worst thing you've done is provided the seed for an interesting conversation.

26

There are two other strong reasons to develop your 10 second elevator speech.

1. It forces you to get very real and very specific about what you do and why you do it. Knowing your BIG WHY will help you develop your elevator speech. Draw upon your background; what did you do before you got into real estate that may be valuable to potential real estate clients (note in the above example the agent had a banking background).

2. If you don't have a good feel for who you want to work with and why, it will have the same effect as marrying any Joe Blow just because they asked you to. Sure in the beginning you may feel like you can't turn down any business and there is a certain logic to that but you will want to learn sooner rather than later what type of client you prefer to work with and why.

The elevator speech is not a new concept. But I do believe it is not emphasized enough by firms and woefully underused by agents. We'll talk more about developing your elevator speech in Chapter 3.

Before we venture much further down this real estate trail, I think it is important that we talk about the most dreaded fear new agents have… PROSPECTING! Indulge me for a few moments and let's see if there really is a Big Foot we should be afraid of.

There is no such thing as Big Foot OR laying to rest a prospecting myth

> Prospect from the Latin *prospectus* view, <u>prospect</u>, from *prospicere* to look forward, exercise foresight, from *pro-* forward + *specere* to look. First Known Use: 15th century

To prospect then may be interpreted to mean: To look for something or someone and to look forward in time; to exercise foresight and anticipate potential customers' needs. To a real estate agent prospecting means to find buyers and sellers, to ask questions about their concerns, their fears and their wants, needs, and housing desires and then help them solve their problem.

Throughout this book you will read about the importance of prospecting. In my opinion, it is a critical element of this business. Eventually buyers and sellers will come to you through referrals and past clients. Even then though you will need to regularly remind people you're in this business to help people buy and sell homes. But in the beginning, particularly in the beginning, you must regularly seek out buyers and sellers. You will see that I recommend you contact members of your circle of influence regularly. I encourage you to reach out to them in the hope that they know someone looking to buy or sell a home and I layout guidelines for prospecting and scripts for prospecting.

The myth I want to put to rest though is not the need to prospect – of that there is no question – but in the way you go about it. It doesn't matter whether you follow my advice or you create your own system. What does matter is that you regularly seek out buyers and sellers. The traditional prospecting method of calling people to ask, *"Who do you know that is looking to buy or sell a home?"* is passé, unrewarding, and downright drudgery. If you don't see yourself picking up the phone and dialing for dollars then don't do it… But you must do something, anything that raises your profile and makes the public aware that you are in this business to help people buy and sell real estate. And because their

28

memories are short, you must do it regularly and frequently. If you don't, I can assure you, you will exit this business as quietly as you entered it.

While on this journey you will receive innumerable amounts of advice and counsel regarding growing your business. In fact there is a plethora of books espousing the need to prospect, but just as many that purport you don't need to prospect at all. Some suggest you can blog your way to success while others offer a myriad of pre-canned letters you can mail. There are farming strategies, automated mailers and marketing trinkets by the truckload. The strategies for building your business may all differ on what you do or don't need to do, but I can guarantee that they all agree on one thing – **consistency**. No matter what you do you must be consistent and perform that action on a regular basis. Only you are going to know what methods work best to help you get your name out there. Find them, pick out the ideas you feel comfortable with and implement them. But do not dismiss prospecting or the need to do it consistently as an evil, cheap or underhanded way of conducting business. Prospecting, simply put, is nothing more than personally advertising yourself and instead of waiting for customers to come into your store, you take your store to them.

Prospecting does not have to be the big scary thing nearly every agent perceives it to be. Remember, the above definition can be read to mean: Look for people and look forward to anticipate needs. How you get yourself out there is up to you, just be sure you do it regularly.

If the word prospecting gives you chills and causes you to shudder at the mere thought of having to do it, here are other words equivalent to it: View, Scene, Vision, Outlook, Panorama, Vista, Hope, Possibility, Likelihood, Probability, and Potential. So if prospecting is unsettling to you then why not refer to it as a "vista with great potential..."

Oh, and if a real estate firm has a certain *vista with great potential* requirement that you simply do not see yourself doing, you will most likely want to look for a different firm.

29

Trail Log:

Chapter 5: Laying in your provisions OR the hardware and software needed and not needed.

What to fill your pack with OR the hardware you will need

Let's start with what's not needed. You do not need a brand new computer, an iPad, a copier, fax machine, 27 inch monitor, recording pen that records spoken words along with what you write (yes they have them and yes they are very cool). You do not need a new car, a GPS (unless you're directionally challenged or new to the area. Even then I'll explain why you shouldn't need one). You do not need the latest in video recording gear, a digital voice recorder, a laser measuring device. Finally you do not need a Supra-Key or Lockbox unless you have a buyer or seller; more about these two items below.

Hardware you need:

1. A reliable **desktop or laptop computer**. Most of your work will be internet based so be sure it can connect to Wi-Fi using a T1 connection or wirelessly.

2. A **smart phone**. It does not have to be the latest but should not be more than one level back.

3. **Business cards** with your photo.
    I hate cameras and honestly they hate me but I have my picture on the card because it's easier to put a face to a name and vice versa. I suggest you put your picture on your business cards. However, be mindful of going for the glamour shots; honestly, what business are we in? Simply dress professionally and take a nice picture. After you have been in the business awhile, be sure to update your photo. Let's face it; you probably don't look like the you of 10 years ago and 10 years from now you won't look like the you of today. Whether you'll rejoice in this or not depends entirely on your DNA and the clients you've chosen to work for.

31

Be careful about using gloss finished cards, they are difficult to write on and the recipient may just want to jot a few notes on the card you just gave them.

With this in mind, you may want to consider leaving the back of the card blank. I have seen the backs of many business cards state the following, *"I love referrals. The greatest compliment I can receive is the referral of your friends and family."* Or words to that affect. My goodness, doesn't that go without saying? If you feel you need to put something on the back of your card, why not write out a summary of your 10 second elevator speech (see Chapter Six) so the recipient knows exactly who you are looking for and how they can help you find them.

Better yet, create a YouTube video of yourself and then generate a QR code that is on the back of your business card. Wow, a video business card! (See resources for more on QR codes).

4. An inexpensive portable **hanging folder box** to keep in your car. In it you should keep buyer and seller packages containing the various forms you need. I am not going to try to explain what should be in those folders because it depends on what you decide to specialize in. In general though the following should be in every folder:

    –   Working with Real Estate Agents Brochure
    –   Agency agreements for both buyers and sellers
    –   Sample contracts and addenda
    –   Actual contracts and addenda
    –   Any necessary disclosure forms
    –   Agent Compensation and Representation form
    –   Listing checklist
    –   Buyer checklist
    –   MLS data input sheet

Your firm should provide you a list of forms they want you to have on hand.

↑ Remember, opportunity does not come to those who wait or pray; it comes to those who are prepared to walk through the door that has just been opened... Be prepared with a folder that contains all of the documents you need for buyers and sellers.

5. **Realtor pin and company name tag**. I must admit when I first entered the business I wore neither of them. I'm not sure why; maybe I felt a bit nerdy wearing them. Now that I've been in the business lo these many years, I wear both proudly. After all if you're not proud to be a Realtor why are you in the business? Interestingly, now that I wear them I can't tell you the number of times I've been standing in line at a local coffee house and the person in front of me turns and strikes up a conversation about real estate. I've handed out business cards, enlarged my contact list, received referral business and accepted invitations to meet with my new friends to talk about listing their properties. All because I wore a lapel pin...

↑ The Realtor pin and your company name tag are one of the best forms of advertising and they are most likely free of cost.

6. **Magnet sign for your car**. I think it can help grow your business and they are not that expensive. With the creation of QR codes, I believe the sign can now be even more effective. Although if you're at a stop light, don't assume the person in the car next to you is taking your picture, she may simply be scanning your QR code to see what it does. I have never seen a magnet get stolen from a car and I've never seen them cause rust.

7. **A printer**. A black and white laser is more than adequate for the vast majority of your needs. A color printer looks nice but can get expensive with ink or color laser refills. If it is ink based and you use it to create those pretty color flyers you're going to stick

in the brochure box at your first listing, you will learn quickly and regrettably how just a little bit of morning dew can make those colors bleed. In general black and white copies in the brochure box are more than adequate. Should you need a printer, I suggest you invest in a 3-in-1 printer/fax/scanner. Fax machines are slowly going the way of the Dodo bird but they are still used. Your scanner though will be used frequently to scan and email documents.

8. **Supra Key and lockboxes**. I advise my agents to purchase a Supra Key and one lockbox and put the lockbox in their living room next to their sign (yes they have signs in their living rooms). Why? Well how long are you going to want to look at a sign and lockbox sitting in your living room, den or bedroom? Once you have your first listing and you've put the sign and lockbox out, go purchase another sign and lockbox and rinse and repeat. With that said though, these items are not immediately critical. Even if you happened to get a listing on your first day or you picked up a buyer on your second, a quick trip to the Realtor store and your firm's storage room puts everything right.

9. **A 100 foot tape measure, graph paper, and cheap clipboard**. You will most likely be measuring your listings so why not purchase a measuring tape and practice on your own and your neighbor's home before you get too busy. (You also have to measure a home as part of the 301 Post Licensing course so buy a 100 foot tape measure sooner rather than later.) Be sure to look on both sides of the tape measure. One side should reflect 10^{ths} of an inch so you can plug that number in your calculator (9 inches is not $9/10^{th}$ it's .75). Finally, remember that the NC RE Commission does not require you to measure homes; that requirement is left up to your local MLS board. But if you do measure the home they will hold you accountable for the accuracy of that measurement. Even if you hire out, the NC RE Commission will still hold you accountable for the measurement's accuracy, you can never absolve yourself of

liability as the listing agent.

I suggest as part of your first week's activity, you practice measuring your home and your neighbor's or friend's home. It is an excellent skill to have and shows that you are a true real estate professional. As an added bonus you will not have to fork out money to pay someone to measure a home. Oh sure, there are certain homes I wouldn't attempt to measure but it's a good bet those homes are in the million dollar plus price range and for those, I'm willing to pay someone to measure the home.

10. **Digital Still/Video Camera**: As inexpensive as digital video cameras are becoming they are a good investment. Smart phones can also take videos, but at this time, I don't think they're high enough quality for virtual tours. Smart phones can also take pictures and I've seen the results in the MLS – not pretty. Play around with your phone, take pictures of your home and see what it can do. If necessary buy a digital camera and/or digital video camera.

11. **Cars**. I love my car. It's a 1999 Toyota Camry. It's a clean and reliable car with almost 250,000 miles on it. Would I be ashamed to put a buyer in it? No way! I've done it many times and they've never once complained that they're not riding in a brand new BMW or Mercedes. Keep your car clean and reliable. You'll be fine for the foreseeable future.

If, however, you smoke in your car, no amount of cleaning or order eliminating spray will provide relief to a buyer who is allergic to smoke; in fact, these sprays can often irritate their sinuses further. I am not going to provide advice on how to handle this situation because, let's face it, you already know the answer.

12. **GPS systems**. Why are you using a GPS system to find a home you plan to show the buyer with the buyer in your car or following you in their car? Shouldn't you have already scouted

out that home before bringing the buyer to it? My advice, skip the GPS and spend your time and money getting to know the city and your market the old fashioned way... Drive around and learn your market.

The vast majority of buyers begin their home search on the internet and so they will already have directions to the homes they are interested in. Shouldn't you be testing these directions so if there is an error, you can notify the out-of-town buyer before they start driving around? As a professional, should you discover an error or confusion with the directions notify the listing agent so they can correct the problem.

Further, I believe you should see the homes you're going to show buyers before you actually show them. Think about a trail guide, they have reviewed the trails not only from the maps but they have walked them and they know where the dangers are and where the trail gets rough. You are your buyer's trail guide. Preview homes before putting the buyer in your car or you ask them to use their gas to follow you to a home neither one of you like because the listing agent failed to mention the enormous power sub-station just to the left of the photo they took.

Previewing homes will make you a better and more informed agent. You will understand your market better and when you are in a conversation with someone who is describing their ideal home that happens to match the one you just previewed that morning you may be able to create one very satisfied buyer.

Previewing homes also makes you a more confident agent because you know your inventory better and can speak more intelligently about the market, the trends in the market, market prices and what areas are hot and which are cool. Have you ever struggled with locating a particular item while shopping at a large store and one clerk says, *"I don't know did you check aisle 12? If it's not there we don't carry it."* While another clerk says, *"We do carry that item. It used to be on aisle 12 but it's now on the end cap of aisle 3. Let me take you to it. By the way we have it in blue now do you have a color preference?"* Now really, who would you rather work with and if they were commissioned based, who would get the sale?

↑ Know your inventory. It is the essence of your business!

What trail mix do you need OR necessary software

Just like the gear you carry into the woods, what you put in your body is just as important. There are hundreds if not thousands of software products out there. All of them claim they'll make you a better agent, more successful and even better looking.

1. **Client database products:** Top Producer, Constant Contact, Primasoft, Sage ACT, Realty Juggler and the list goes on and on. In my opinion you do not need any kind of client tracking system early in your career accept for maybe the one your future firm provides. First of all, you probably aren't going to have a list of hundreds or thousands of names and if you do you probably are already tracking them with a software product.

   Secondly, these products can be very robust and full of bells and whistles. If you aren't careful you can spend hours playing with all these bells and whistles and accomplishing little actual productive work. Finally, these products can be expensive. Starting out you need to be frugal with your money and for every dollar you spend you need to see at least a dollar in return. My advice is to stick to the basics and grow into these products organically. As your business grows you will have a much better understanding of the products that will help you be more productive.

2. **Calendar software:** You may keep your calendar in an old fashioned notebook or (as my father does) on index cards or you may utilize the latest calendaring software tool. In any case, I urge you to maintain only one calendar. Should you keep more

37

than one calendar, I promise you at some point you will create conflicting meetings and you will have to choose between your son's first football game and a listing appointment (choose your son's football game.).

3. **Microsoft Office:** Most of us are familiar with Microsoft Office and I'm going to speak to this product because it is the most commonly used but there are other products (some internet based) that offer the same features for free or at a reduced cost. With that said, I do believe you need to be proficient in:

    Microsoft Word: A word processing software program that is used to create and edit documents and various kinds of printed communications. A very useful product and if you are uncomfortable with using a personal computer this product is the foundation for much of the software in use today. Learn Microsoft Word and its offerings and you can master virtually all the PC based software out there.

    Microsoft Excel: a spreadsheet program which lets you enter, modify and perform functions on sets of data. Excel is a very useful tool for tracking your contact database, listings, sales numbers, etc… it is almost limitless in its ability to manipulate data.

    Microsoft Publisher: Enables you to create a myriad of publications, from brochures to magazines or marketing material; very powerful and fun to use. However, be careful you don't find yourself having so much fun you become a publisher or marketing designer instead of a real estate agent.

A word of caution… Once you become proficient with the world of software, you may find yourself playing, tweaking and generally puttering on your computer. Resist the urge! Your personal computer and all its trappings are a tool; use them wisely and frugally so most of your time is spent with the people who can help you grow your business.

4. **Email address:** The Company you join will most likely provide you with an email address. I believe you should use it for all email communication. Your email address is a way to remind recipients that you sell real estate and it projects a professional image. An email transmitted by SuzyQ22345@yahoo.com is not going to carry the same professional weight as Suzy@AbcRealty.com. If you are concerned about having to check multiple email systems, you can use a product like Microsoft Outlook that allows all of your emails to be viewed and transmitted from one window. Remember we sell relationships so it is important to project the right image.

 Always have a signature line on your outgoing emails. The signature line allows you to place your company's logo, your cell phone number, Facebook icon, Twitter icon, etc... Set up your signature line during your first week.

5. **Website**: Should your firm allow you to create your own domain name for your website or page on their website, please remember that visitors to your site will have to type the name in. If you choose www.TerryWilsonSellsLotsofCharlotteRealEstateHomes.com that is a lot to remember and a lot of typing. On the other hand if I choose www.TWSLCREH.com that doesn't tell them anything. Chose your domain name carefully and if possible, be sure it reflects the essence of your 10 second elevator speech.

6. **Videos, Movies, Video Tours**: Should you decide to do video blogs or other videos, be sure the camera comes with software that allows you to easily transfer the videos to your computer and the internet. Microsoft offers a free version of MovieMaker and there is a plethora of free video making software on the internet. Play around with them and learn how to make your own

movies that you can upload to the internet. Better yet, take a class so you quickly master the features of these products and produce quality movies from the beginning. Producing movies has gotten so easy I really don't see a need to hire a professional.

Virtual tours can be an effective way to show the home to interested buyers via the internet. However, interested buyers are not the only ones looking at the home. People with bad intentions have been known to use virtual tours to get a lay of the land before they rob the home. Consider carefully what you will include in the virtual tour and be extra cautious when it comes to children's playrooms and bedrooms. I see no reason to take pictures and certainly no videos of these rooms.

7. **Blogs:** A blog is a web-log it is essentially an online diary or a place for you to regularly share your thoughts. When blogging first came on the scene everyone wanted to read them and write them. Like everything on the internet, things can quickly become saturated. Blogs are still popular but they have become as common as digital watches – cool and unique at one time but now ordinary and mundane. But what of that digital watch that also acts as a cell phone; now there is something to talk about. What I'm trying to say is that if your blog isn't refreshing and unique it will be sparsely followed (at least initially) and will not be subject to going viral – in which thousands and millions look forward to your musings, and that's just fine. You can still create a blog and use it to help you establish credibility. As with anything you want to sell, you should advertise and talk about your blog so people will want to follow you. Finally, here are a few important tips to remember:

🖥 If you start blogging, you should be consistent. If you create a blog today and then not share your witticisms for a month, don't expect a lot of followers. Blog creation needs to be part of your daily or at least weekly marketing efforts.

▭ You don't have to create all of your blogs. You can, for example, read an interesting article or another individual's blog and point to their blog in your blog. You're happy because they did the work for you, they're happy because someone else is reading their blog and your followers are happy because you provided them much needed information. Win-Win-Win!! Remember you don't have to be the source of all information, simply be the source of the source.

▭ When I was young, my mother would prepare huge meals on the weekend and then freeze them for ready to eat meals during the week. It made her life a little easier (I say "a little" because she did have me as a son after all.). Make your life easier by creating a series of blogs that you can copy and paste throughout the week. By the way, if you plan to Tweet on Twitter.com you can use this technique there too.

▭ Numbered lists are great for blogging (or Tweeting for that matter) because you can dole them out daily or weekly and just like cliff hangers in old movies, they'll keep your readers coming back for more. (For example: 10 Biggest Mistakes Buyers Make, or Five Critical Steps You Must Take Before Getting a Loan, or Three Inexpensive Repairs That Will Make Your Home Show Better.) That is 18 days or 18 weeks of blog posts right there!!

▭ Don't worry if no one is following you. In the truest sense, blogs are the classic *"if you build it they will come."* As with everything, the cream will rise to the top and well thought out blogs will be followed. The purpose of your blog isn't solely to get millions of followers to hang on your every word (although that would be a very nice way to create an endless supply of potential leads). It also serves to force you to stay up with the latest trends and marketing changes and economic fluctuations in real estate. Blogs also serve as a way for you to come across as the expert in your field. If someone asks you a real estate question you've blogged about, of course, you will answer their

41

question but you will also have the opportunity to steer them to your blog for further reference on the subject and create a follower.

 Review Appendix B for a checklist of your first week's activities.

Trail Log:

_____

_____

_____

_____

_____

_____

_____

_____

_____

_____

_____

_____

_____

_____

_____

_____

_____

_____

_____

_____

_____

_____

_____

_____

Chapter 6: Seeing the end of the trail in your mind's eye OR setting and accomplishing your goals.

> *"82% of agents said their biggest mistakes, upon entering the business, were not goal setting, not planning, not prospecting enough and not following up consistently."* 2010 NAR study

If you want to be a successful, well respected, well compensated and a life balanced agent. Do those things that 82% of agents don't do!!

Before beginning this exercise, read through it a couple of times to become familiar with it; then work the exercise…

Although goals can be an effective way to hold yourself accountable and help you accomplish something they aren't the end all and be all. A poor goal simply means you held yourself accountable and accomplished "something" that did you little good or wasn't clear. For example should you say, *"I want to be the best real estate agent in my market."* you're either setting yourself up for failure or you've already achieved success. What do you mean by *"the best"*? Best at what, how is it measurable? In fact, one could argue, that you're already the best; it's just that nobody knows it yet.

Seeing the trail's end OR why create a goal
The Cheshire cat from "Alice in Wonderland" said it best…

> *"'Cheshire Puss,' she began, rather timidly, as she did not at all know whether it would like the name: however, it only grinned a little wider. `Come, it's pleased so far,' thought Alice, and she went on. `Would you tell me, please, which way I ought to go from here?' 'That depends a good deal on where you want to get to,' said the Cat. `I don't much care where--' said Alice. `Then it doesn't matter which way you go,' said the Cat. `--so long as I get SOMEWHERE,' Alice added as an*

43

explanation `Oh, you're sure to do that,' said the Cat, `if you only walk long enough.'"

— Excerpted from Alice in Wonderland
By Lewis Carroll

Without a goal, Alice would certainly "get somewhere" but where and to what end? Starting a career in real estate without having at least a semblance of a goal is the same as entering a trail head on the AT without knowing where it leads… Sure you'll get somewhere but it may not be where you want to be.

Why does goal setting work?
By nature we are goal setting creatures. The problem is the goals we set and accomplish each day are done so often they no longer feel like goals, so we forget what motivates us.

For example: You've joined a firm and it is Tuesday morning. Your goal this morning is to arrive at the Tuesday morning sales meeting. Think about the many steps you took to accomplish this. What other goals do you have today that you may not even realize are goals: shopping, cleaning, napping etc…)? Think about the days you accomplished your to-do list; didn't you feel better?

I believe another reason goal setting works is that once you begin working toward a goal you reach a point where you simply are no longer willing to give up on the goal because you have invested too much of yourself and your time. Whatever you think of this book - and I hope you think well of it - it is something I had considered doing for quite some time but never took action. I finally sat down and made it a SMART goal (more on this later) and began writing. After putting in over 30 hours of my time I found myself compelled to finish it. I was not going to simply waste 30 hours of writing time.

Building a roaring campfire OR how to create goals

Five principles of goal setting (by Dr. Edwin Locke)
Dr. Edwin Locke's comments are in quotes.

1. **Clarity**. Goals have to be clear and Dr. Locke suggests the SMART methodology (more on this in a moment)

2. **Challenge**: "It's important to strike an appropriate balance between a challenging goal and a realistic goal. Setting a goal that you'll fail to achieve is possibly more de-motivating than setting a goal that's too easy. The need for success and achievement is strong; therefore people are best motivated by challenging, but realistic, goals. Ensuring that goals are Achievable or Attainable is one of the elements of SMART."

3. **Commitment**. You have to want it! How often have you worked toward a goal someone else has set for you without buying into it yourself? (As Dr. Phil says, *"How's that working out for you?"*).

   ⚑ Do not set a goal that you do not want. You will be uncommitted and you will only be setting yourself up for failure.

4. **Feedback**: It has often been said that if you can't measure it you can't track it. I suppose that's true. Most successful AT "through hikers" set daily mileage goals and use maps and trail markers to track how they're doing. After all, you do not want to be at the Northern Terminus in Maine as February's winter rage is about to unfold. You need to track your mileage and adjust accordingly as you go to assure you are making not just good progress, but the correct amount of progress necessary to finish your hike at the right time. In real estate then, your goal has to be specific enough so you can track your progress toward it.

45

5.   **Task complexity:** "Give yourself time to accomplish the goal and don't make it overly complex."

Setting goals the SMART way

Specific:

A specific goal has a much greater chance of being accomplished rather than a general goal because a specific goal gives you a clear picture of what you are trying to accomplish. It is the difference between saying, *"Starting at mile post 218, I will walk 22 miles on the AT today and rest at mile post 230 arriving at mile post 240 by 6 PM to set up camp before dark."* As opposed to *"I'll walk as far as I can today."*

To set a specific goal you must answer the six "W" questions:

1.   **Who**: Who is involved? (I.e. who can help me accomplish my goal? Hint: Initially, it's your circle of influence.)
2.   **What**: What do I want to accomplish?
3.   **Where**: Identify a location. (You cannot be an expert on your entire real estate market inclusive of all price ranges in all areas from single family homes to commercial property... Get specific. Find your niche.)
4.   **When**: It is important to establish a time frame. Having an open-ended time frame is nothing but a built-in excuse to never accomplish your goal. There is even a button you can wear called "a round tu-it" because you'll get around to it someday. When discussing how to prepare for pre-license final exams, I sometimes hear students say that they prefer to cram for the final exam. Study after study clearly indicates that cramming for an exam is not as effective as regular study habits that steadily march toward the goal of passing the exam. The reason many of them study best by cramming is because this is the only time they study – it is not uncommon that they fail. It is important that you establish a clear objective and then identify bench marks along the way to assure you are making consistent and steady progress toward your goal and if not, you can make adjustments before it is too late.
5.   **Which**: Identify requirements and constraints.

6. **Why**: Specific reasons, purpose or benefits of accomplishing the goal. (You guessed it… the BIG WHY.)

Let's look at another example of a specific goal:

A general goal might be, *"I want to put a house under contract by the end of the year."* But a specific goal that is focused and clear would say, *"I will assist a first time home buyer client in the purchase of a home priced in the $150,000 to $200,000 price range and close on that home no later than December 31st."*

By having a specific goal you know exactly what you need to do to accomplish it so you can target your marketing and your daily efforts like a laser. You can share this goal with your circle of influence so they know exactly what they need to do to assist you in accomplishing it. And you clearly know whether you achieved your goal or not.

You may argue that the first goal also allows us to see whether we accomplished it or not (i.e. put a house under contract) and you make a reasonable point but if the contract falls through did you still achieve a goal that will sustain you?

Measurable:

"Establish concrete criteria for measuring progress toward the attainment of each goal you set. When you measure your progress, you stay on track, reach your target dates, and experience the exhilaration of achievement that spurs you on to continued effort required to reach your goal. To determine if your goal is measurable, ask questions such as: How much? How many? How will I know when it is accomplished?"

Attainable:

"When you identify goals that are most important to you, you begin to figure out ways you can make them come true. You develop the attitudes, abilities, skills, and financial capacity to reach them. You begin seeing previously overlooked opportunities to bring yourself closer to the achievement of your goals.

You can attain most any goal you set when you plan your steps wisely and establish a time frame that allows you to carry out those steps. Goals that may have seemed far away and out of reach eventually move closer and become attainable, not because your goals shrink, but because you grow and expand to match them. When you establish your goals you build your self-image. You see yourself as worthy of these goals, and develop the traits and personality that allow you to possess them."

Realistic/Relevant:
"To be realistic, a goal must represent an objective toward which you are both willing and able to work. A goal can be both high and realistic; you are the only one who can decide just how high your goal should be. But be sure that every goal represents substantial progress. A high goal is frequently easier to reach than a low one because a low goal exerts low motivational force. Some of the hardest jobs you ever accomplished actually seem easy simply because they were a labor of love (i.e. they were relevant). Low goals tend to become unimportant to you. The consequence of not accomplishing a low goal (even one that is relevant) does not cause enough "pain" to push you to accomplish it.
Your goal is probably realistic if you truly believe that it can be accomplished. Additional ways to know if your goal is realistic is to determine if you have accomplished anything similar in the past or ask yourself what conditions would have to exist to accomplish this goal."

I must admit, I am not overly motivated by establishing lofty goals; in fact I tend to become fatalistic if the goal is too high. However, I draw great motivation by exceeding the goal I create… Simply put, I am more motivated by passing the goal and watching it fade into the distance in my rearview mirror than I am by seeing a large goal in front of me that I must surmount. That is me though; your goal and your motivation are yours. You must, however, have a goal and strive toward it (or, as with me, away from it).

⚑ Be careful about joining a firm that sets goals for you. I talk with my agents about setting goals but I always preface the conversation with these words, *"My goals are my goals; they*

48

are not your goals." No one can dictate what your goals are. Hopefully the goals you wish to achieve are in line with the firm's and if so, you have an excellent match. Finally, a goal has to be <u>relevant</u> to you. It has to have meaning. You have to want it!

Timely/Tangible:

A goal should be grounded within a time frame. With no time frame there is no sense of urgency. If you want to lose 10 pounds, when do you want to lose it by? Someday won't work. But if you anchor it within a timeframe, "by May 1st", then you have set your subconscious mind into motion to begin working on that goal.

T "can also stand for Tangible – A goal is tangible when you can experience it with one of the senses, that is, taste, touch, smell, sight or hearing."

When your goal is tangible you have a better chance of making it specific and measurable and thus attainable. (For example: see yourself at the closing table, visualize yourself sitting with the seller as they sign the listing agreement, see yourself putting the sign in the yard. Smell your commission check, etc...)

On the next few pages are guides to help you establish, track and accomplish your goals:

- Long term goal setting guide.
- Creating a SMART goal with signatures.
- Weekly tracking chart.

Speaking of goals, why not create a SMART goal to finish this book and all its exercises?

Long term goal setting guide

We don't always know what our goals are or if they are achievable. Read through this exercise and use it to help you focus in on your goals.

Your three year goal:

I prefer looking out no more than three years because I can't see five years down the road. It simply is too far to realistically envision where I want to be and what I want to accomplish. However, three years is a horizon I can just barely see.

Regarding your personal life and your real estate career, what are three things you want to accomplish?

3 year real estate career goals	3 year personal life goals
1.	1.
2.	2.
3.	3.

Take a look at these goals. Do they mesh? In other words, if you say you want to spend more time with your family (which isn't very measurable by the way) but you also want to sell $100 million in real estate per year by your third year, something is going to have to give.

Your goals are your goals, just make sure they mesh and can work harmoniously together.

One year goals:

Now drop back to your one year. Based on your three year goals where do you need to be by the end of your first year?

One year real estate career goals	One year personal life goals
1.	1.
2.	2.
3.	3.

Creating these goals:

This is all well and good but how do I go about creating these goals? We'll get to that in a second. First though, your goals must follow the SMART methodology as discussed above.

Bad Goal: *"By the end of my first year, I want to be the top producer in all of Lake Norman."*

Ok, this might be Time oriented but is it specific? Is it Measurable? Is it Attainable? I argue that it is none of these. "Top producer" is not terribly specific, if it's not specific it's not measurable and although you may be ambitious, is it attainable to be the top producing agent in all of the Lake Norman market in your first year, maybe or maybe not. Even if it is attainable, will it mesh with your personal life goals? Something will most likely have to give.

SMART Goal: *"By the first anniversary of my license, I will close $3,000,000 in residential real estate."* Or, *"By the end of my first year I will earn $55,000 in gross commissions, working 10 hour days 5 days per week."*

Either of these goals is much more measurable, attainable, realistic, and specific and, of course, time oriented.

Creating your goals:

I can't tell you what your goals should be. I can tell you that your family, significant others and friends can help. Start by sitting in a quiet place and close your eyes. When you're feeling relaxed, start thinking further and further out… tomorrow, next week, next month, next year and so on.

51

Go out as far as you realistically can. What are you thinking about? It really doesn't matter; simply try to project what is going on in your life as far down the road as you can. This may take some time and practice but keep at it. Once you have a reasonable idea of what you see, use the upcoming page's exercise to lay out your SMART goal and create buy-in. Discuss this picture with those who are important to you. Do they agree? If so, use this picture to begin establishing the above three year goals for both your personal and business life that help you paint the above picture.

Once you have your three year goals, work backward to determine your one, two and three year goals that will help you achieve it.

NOTE: If you simply cannot envision three years out, go as far as you can. There is certainly nothing wrong with establishing one year goals each year and striving toward them!

SMART Goal Commitment Letter

State Your Specific Goal in the Present Tense
By stating your goal in the present tense, you activate your mind to start focusing on the things, people and opportunities that will help you achieve your goal. You can also repeat this goal statement to yourself daily to help program your mind for success.

The date is: _____ and I: (fill in your name) _____

_____

What will you do to celebrate your goal?
Every goal worth pursuing requires a suitable reward for the hard work that you put into it. How will you reward yourself?

_____

_____

Name your Accountability Advocate(s):
Having someone there to hold your hand and at the same time push you is essential in helping you accomplish your goal. No one walks alone...

By signing this contract, I agree to advocate for the goal owner by regularly checking up on and encouraging the above named person.

Advocate one: _____ Date: _____
Advocate two: _____ Date: _____
Advocate three: _____ Date: _____

By signing this contract, I promise to give myself and my goal 100% of my commitment, dedication and heart and I will see my goal through to its completion.

Goal Owner: _____ Date: _____

Weekly Tracking Chart

Day	What did I do toward my goal Today	What can I do to improve?	What grade would I give myself?	Did I talk with my Accountability Advocate?	Is this goal still important to me?
1					
2					
3					
4					
5					
6					

Action steps:

Now that you have your one, two and three year goals focus on the first year goal. If you want to close three million dollars in residential sales, what are the things you must do to accomplish that?

What is your target market? You could sell a three million dollar home at the beginning of your year and then take a long vacation; but is that realistic, probably not. Although I do remember one memorable transaction in which a brand new agent, while working on phone duty – a task in which she answered the company's main line in hopes of finding business – received a phone call from a buyer interested in purchasing a $2.5 million dollar home. She met the buyer at the house, wrote the offer and the seller accepted it. In her very first transaction, after being on the job for only one week, she cleared $40,000! Sadly, she thought it would always be this easy and within one year she was out of the business for lack of another transaction.

So where do we begin? If you want to sell $3 million of residential real estate in your first year consider the following questions (there are NO wrong answers)...

- What price range do you prefer to work in?
- Do you like resale, new construction, fixer-uppers, and/or foreclosures?
- Do you like investors or owner occupant buyers or putting signs in yards for sellers?
- Do you like first time home buyers or would you prefer working with people who have sold numerous times?
- Do you like working with older or younger people or people your age, men, women, blue collar, or white collar?
- Do you like the country or working in the city?
- How do you feel about driving buyers around?
- Do you like getting dirty or would you rather stay clean and dress up each day?
- Do you prefer to be more like Superman (the hero) or more like Clark Kent (just doing your job)?

Insert your questions and thoughts here...

_____

_____

_____

_____

_____

_____

_____

Do you get the idea? When you understand what you like to do and what you want to accomplish (always subject to change) then you have a better idea of the steps you need to take and the market you need to target with your advertising to accomplish your goal.

Let's say you discover that you like getting dirty, playing Superman and working with blue collar folks... Well you might consider the following...

- Rural expertise in farm sales
- Investment properties requiring rehab
- Foreclosures requiring rehab
- Short-sales (the home might be clean but the process can be messy!)
- Historic home expertise
- Raw land sales
- First time home-buyers

Once you have a better idea of the market, you can now target your advertising and get a better idea of the amount of work you need to do to accomplish your one year goal.

For example, if you decide to work the first time home-buyer market (a very noble and honorable market I might add), most first time home buyers are going to spend between $125,000 and $175,000. If you want to close three million dollars in residential sales your first year, you will need to sell approximately 20 homes (based on average price of $150,000). Is that realistic? Maybe, but only you know based on how it fits in with your other goals.

If it's not realistic, at least you know and you need to adjust your market, your goals or both.

Establishing your market:
- Answer the questions above and add your own as you see fit.

- Once that's done, consider the market(s) that align with your answers.

- Does that market help you achieve your goal?

  - If yes, what amount of effort will you need to expend in that market to achieve your goal?
  - If no, well then you either have to change your goal or change your market...

Marketing
Now that you have an idea of your goals and your desired market(s) how do you go after them (check off each box as you complete the task)?

Start by thinking like them. If it is first time homebuyers, where might they be shopping?
Answer:
- Zillow.com
- Realtor.com
- Trulia.com
- Scores of other websites.

Go to where they are, set up your profile, start monitoring and answering questions daily. In addition, consider the following activities:

- ☐ Establish a Facebook business page and start writing SHORT posts about the home buying or selling process.

- ☐ Establish an account on activerain.com or blogspot.com and start writing blogs about the home buying process.

- ☐ Offer to conduct an informal seminar on the home buying and selling process in a starter home neighborhood's HOA meeting.

- ☐ Contact credit restoration companies/agencies and let them know you would like to conduct a seminar for their clients on how to buy their first home once their credit is restored. Or you would like to stop in and learn more about the credit restoration process so that you can better advise your clients.

- ☐ It goes without saying that you should let *all* your friends and family know what your area of expertise is, so they can be on the lookout for you.
    - o With this in mind, why not spend a little money and create business cards that have your elevator speech on them (or a link to your website or online video) that you can give to your friends and family to remind them of the market you seek.

Your marketing ideas:

_____

_____

_____

_____

Take a second look at the above list, other than the ideas you may have added and the cost of some business cards, what is the total cost? ZERO dollars. But the impact can be tremendous!

I know what you're thinking, *"Terry, I just got in the business, I don't know anything about the first time home buying process."* I understand, but since you didn't have to spend any money on advertising, you can now spend it on books, research, classes and seminars to learn more about it. Even without that, you are already well ahead of buyers and sellers because you have a real estate license.

 Read through this goal setting guide a couple of times and then sit down and establish your goals.

The call of the wild OR your 10 second elevator speech

I admit I am not a fisherman. Sure, when I was a kid I'd put a worm on a hook and catch a few fish but I wasn't serious about it. Although I did hook an eel one time; they are terrific fighters and even more so when you try to throw them back. Real estate is very much like fishing. You can throw an ad out there, hand out a few business cards and you'll probably catch an occasional fish. But if you're a serious bass fisherman you're going to practice your craft regularly and use very specific bait to lure that large-mouth bass out of its hiding place so you can set the hook.

Now that you have an idea of the market your want, it is critical that you create a short, clear and concise message for that market to lure them out so they'll take the bait.

Let's take a look at good and bad bait…

Bad: *"Hi, you should work with me because I provide great customer service and I really care about people. And I love referrals."* Really, what real estate agent doesn't want this?

Instead: *"Hi, I am a foreclosure expert. It is the area I specialize in and as such, I can assure you that I understand the paperwork and documentation banks require assuring a smooth transaction and a greater likelihood of acceptance of a buyer's offer."*

Or: *"Hi, I'm a first time home buyer expert. My primary client base is first time home buyers because I remember what it was like to buy my first home. I understand the amount of paperwork involved, the five lending traps that cause these buyer's loans to fall through and other pitfalls first time home buyers experience. I look for first time home buyers who have struggled to buy a home before but failed. Would you happen to know of anyone that would benefit from this service?"*

I guess you're curious about the "five lending traps" first time home buyers should avoid. So am I so let's go talk to a lender and create that list. Remember you don't have to have the answers; you only need to know who does.

Structuring your 10 second elevator speech
Your 10 second elevator speech gives you the opportunity to clearly convey:

☐ What you do specifically.

☐ Why you do it.

☐ Who you can help as a result of what you do.

☐ How you can help them – your lure. Consider two lures to entice them to take the bait. (i.e. *"5 lending mistakes"* or *"Short Sale expert with a history of success"* or *"Housewife who understands the needs of new mothers buying homes".*) Your life experiences will play a role in how you can help buyers and sellers. Do not dismiss your work history, or lack thereof, when creating your lures…

▪ _____

▪ _____

☐ Why you can help them.

If desired you can add to your elevator speech:

☐   What company you work for.

☐   What is your and/or your company's experience?

What else might you add to your elevator speech?

_____

_____

_____

It is important that you practice your speech until it rolls off your tongue. How will you know? When you can look at yourself in the mirror and say your 10 second elevator speech without flinching or feeling awkward, I'd say you're there.

You may want to have more than one elevator speech depending on who you're talking with. Family members may get one speech while friends get another and strangers get still another. Or you may specialize in more than one geographic area or one area of expertise.

There is space on the next page for you to write out your elevator speech.

Spend a few minutes and write out two or three 10 second elevator speeches

Name of speech: _____

_____
_____
_____
_____
_____
_____

Name of speech: _____

_____
_____
_____
_____
_____
_____

Name of speech: _____

_____
_____
_____
_____
_____
_____

Of course everything is subject to change because life regularly throws change-up balls our way; so your elevator speech is always subject to change. But just like mapping out your AT hike, you now have an idea of the direction you want to go, a field guide to help you get there and a way to share your plan with others. Whether you decide to create your own elevator speech or not, remember...

> *"82% of agents said their biggest*
> *mistakes, upon entering the business,*
> *were not goal setting, not planning, not*
> *prospecting enough and not following up*
> *consistently."* NAR study

If you want to be a successful, well respected, well compensated and a life balanced agent. Do those things that 82% of agents don't do!!

You can and will be successful in this industry if:

- ✓ You want it badly enough.
- ✓ You establish SMART goals.
- ✓ You define your market.
- ✓ You clearly and consistently convey your message with an elevator speech.

Remember, you are not required to have a successful real estate career that meets or exceeds your goals, it is optional, but so too is failing.

Trail Log:

Chapter 7: Putting one foot in front of the other OR what you must do regularly.

Ultimately, you alone will hike this trail. I don't care what you are promised from the firms you interview, in the end, you will be the one putting one foot in front of the other. Happily, however, you won't be lonely, just as there are helpful hikers along the AT, you will meet real estate agents and service providers willing to share their advice and counsel. Take advantage of their wisdom and return the favor when you can. But you must remember that at the end of the day, this is your business and everyone is your competitor. They want your business and you better want theirs. Of course, I mean for this competition to be fair and honest, but this business feeds those that are hungry and if you aren't hungry, you will starve. Rather ironic wouldn't you say?

Every day you must remind yourself that you now own a company. You have a bottom line, profit and loss, inventory (or lack thereof), vendors and clients (or, again, lack thereof). Your education is up to you. Your listing and buyer presentation skills are up to you. Your ability to market yourself is, say it with me, up to you.

With this in mind, you need to prepare yourself before launching into your hike. In this chapter we will discuss getting and staying in real estate shape, studying your trail maps and setting up your online presence.

Have you ever lost weight or known a friend who has? Did it happen over night? Did they eat one fantasy meal that resulted in their desired weight loss? I'm guessing not but should you invent that fantasy meal, forget about real estate, you'll be rich beyond your wildest dreams! Getting yourself in trail-ready shape is no different; you must work at it every day with a disciplined, no excuses approach. I find the business of real estate to be rather peculiar because in many ways it is a very simple business – find a buyer interested in buying a home, find that home and write the contract; go to closing and collect your check... simple! Except it's not simple at all because if it were the failure rate wouldn't be astronomical and if it were simple, every active real estate agent would be driving their dream car and living in their dream home and eating, I suppose, their fantasy meal.

> *So what separates the 10% of successful real estate agents from the 90% of unsuccessful ones? The successful ones take a disciplined and no excuses approach to their business.*

Getting in shape

Every week, especially in the beginning, you must:

- Practice presenting the Working with Real Estate Agents Brochure.
- Practice your 10 second elevator speech.
- Study the various contracts and practice filling them in.
- Practice your listing and buyer presentations.

One of the best pieces of advice I ever received from a Broker-in-Charge was to practice my listing presentation and Working with Real Estate Agent Brochure presentation at least once per week. When he suggested this my response was, *"I don't have any buyers and sellers to 'practice' on."* To which he kindly replied, *"You'll either deliver your presentation to a buyer or seller or to me but you'll do it at least once per week."*

Find someone (preferably not a spouse or other family member, trust me) and practice. The last thing you need is to have ignored this very important part of the business for several weeks or months only to have an out-of-the-blue seller contact you to list their home and you are as rusty as a sunken ship.

Also note that I am not saying that your presentation has to be polished using multi-media and high glossy print outs. However, you do need to be able to smoothly and comfortably talk about yourself, your company, the Listing Agreement, the Offer to Purchase and Contract, the Working with Real Estate Agents Brochure and the Buyer's Agency Agreement. You have to be able to comfortably and confidently discuss your Comparable Market Analysis (CMA). And you must strive to be able to explain all of these documents with every-day common language in an easy manner without losing the legal meaning in the language of the contracts. Finally, you may not skip paragraphs in these documents simply because you don't understand them. I've seen agents do it and I reluctantly admit that I have done it too. There is no excuse for not understanding every paragraph in these very important contracts and being able to explain them to your clients clearly and concisely.

- Practice completing the buyer agency, listing agreement and offer to purchase contracts.

As a humorous side note (although it wasn't humorous at the time), my wife bought a beautiful wooden pen for me which I used on one of my very first listings. The only problem was I was nervous and my palms were sweaty. You guessed it; the wooden pen kept slipping out of my hand. Buy an inexpensive pen with a good rubber grip.

Study your maps

Study the MLS for the market territory you desire to work and become familiar with the following:

- How many homes are currently on the market?
  - What are the average days on market?
  - How many are short sales or foreclosures?

- How many homes are pending?

- How many homes sold within the last year? The last 6 months?

- What is the average:
  - Days on Market?
  - List to sale ratio?
  - List price?
  - Sold price?
  - Square footage?

- Study the styles of homes selling (i.e. ranch, 2-story, master up or down, brick or vinyl sided, etc...) then just as importantly ask why? As you think about the answer, you'll begin thinking like buyers and have a much better idea of what they are looking for, their buying habits, and who they are. Just as hunters (human and animal) study the habits of their prey to better locate them, study your potential buyers buying habits and you'll be able to locate them that much easier. I assume I don't need to clarify that we are only talking about marketing to them...

- How many listings expired or were withdrawn? What were their average prices and days on market? If a potential listing falls within this price range, it too may expire or be withdrawn. Do you really want that listing?

Regularly staying on top of this information will make you an extremely well informed agent who can quickly work through the available inventory for a buyer and one who can quickly decide whether a listing is worth taking or not.

Often new agents will jump at any listing they can get their hands on. I suppose the logic is *I may not sell this house but I might pick up a buyer.* True enough. The only problem is that if you take a listing that is clearly over-priced you are not starting your referral business off on the right foot. People appreciate honesty. If you believe it is over-priced, be careful about taking the listing just to get a sign in the yard. I have done it and I have lived to regret it. It left a bad taste in my mouth, it alienated the seller and rarely produced a buyer because – this is especially true today – buyers have a plethora of tools available to them to help them determine whether a home is fairly priced or over-priced. Don't jump at a listing simply to stick a sign in the yard; more often than not you will regret it.

For example: a few months before writing this book I received a phone call to list a property. I visited the seller and explained that his home was not worth what he needed and since he did not need to sell he should not put his home on the market. Two other agents told him he should sell and suggested an over-priced listing (this is known as buying the listing). Three weeks later guess who the seller called? Upon meeting with him a second time I explained where he needed to be priced and that he would most likely be bringing money to the closing table. He agreed and as of this writing we closed on his house. Was he happy to bring money to the closing table? Of course not but he appreciated the honesty and he was satisfied that there were no unpleasant surprises. We had a cordial and professional relationship that left no ill will. And I have no qualms in calling him to ask for referrals or to simply check in.

Acquiring your trail pass OR setting up your online presence

I'm no Nostradamus but I predict the internet is here to stay (I'm very intuitive that way). With that said, let's embrace that buyers and sellers now have at their finger tips nearly the identical information we have through our MLS. There is very little information that we have that they don't have or can't get – even if it requires slightly more effort on their part.

At one time we controlled nearly all of the information. If you wanted a three bedroom two bath home, we decided which ones you would see. Not anymore. Now buyers go to Zillow or Trulia or Realtor.com, or a host of other sites and perform their own searches. Then they walk into our offices or more likely meet us at a Starbucks or even more likely text or email us and tell us exactly what homes they are interested in seeing. They already know if the seller owes back taxes and the school district the home is in. They have a print out of the plat map; they've visited the HOA (Home Owners Association) website and may have even browsed the CC&R's (Conditions, Covenants and Restrictions); they have previewed the home on Google Earth and they have probably googled the subdivision name to see what they can see and visited the county sheriff's website for crime statistics. They've studied the county's Register of Deeds for liens and other recorded documents. If there is a virtual tour they've previewed both the inside and outside of the home and with Google's Street View they've even driven by the home... In other words, they probably know more about the home than we do. And what's really scary is they did this from the comfort of their current residence and they haven't even gotten in the car yet.

What does this mean to us? Well if the buyer and sellers' information gathering party has moved then we should probably move too. I often equate our business to a progressive dinner party. The only problem is we Realtors are still at the home serving the main course (our MLS) while the buyers and sellers have moved off to the house serving dessert. We better get in our cars and drive to the dessert home soon or who knows where they'll go next!

Where are the buyers and sellers eating their dessert?
- Facebook.com
- Linkedin.com
- Zillow.com
- Homes.com
- Trulia.com
- Realtor.com
- Yahoo.com
- Youtube.com
- Rateyouragent.com
- Twitter.com
- And a thousand new websites coming to a computer near you.

The internet is the new frontier and I need to be blunt with you... If you are not comfortable with a computer. Get comfortable. It's as necessary and common place as your home phone - assuming you still have one which most millennials don't...

In fact, not only do they not have home phones, they think email is passé. What's worse (or better if you're on top of your game) is that in a recent study members of the Millennial generation (AKA Generation Y, Generation Next, Net Generation, Echo Boomers) were asked when they felt they would purchase a home; two thirds indicated that it would be within the next five years (from 2011). Who are the Millennials? They

70

are the baby boom generation's children. There is not a specific age range although some historians have placed them as being born between 1983 and 2005. Regardless of when they were born, many are coming of age and they are the largest pool of potential buyers out there.

Most were born with an Atari 2600® or newer gaming system in their hand, a desktop PC or a laptop to play with and many were born with a Blackberry® clipped to their diapers and to them the idea of email is passé. They prefer text messages and they prefer a response to their text message immediately. They use acronyms that change regularly (remember when LOL meant Lots of Love?). They browse the internet and locate what they need as easily and certainly much faster as baby boomers used to do using the Yellow Pages.

During the writing of this book, I had lunch at fast food restaurant and I was chatting with a woman in line – yes I had my Realtor pin on and yes it was what kicked the conversation off – as we talked, I noticed her toddler son, who was three or maybe four years old, playing with an IPhone®. I pointed out that her child might drop her IPhone and she replied, *"Oh no, that's his. He loves to Facetime his grandpa on it and plays his games."* Whoa… how will this toddler be communicating 20 years from now when he's ready to buy his first home?

What's a Realtor to do? Catch up if you aren't there yet. Embrace the ever changing communication styles and methods. Do not be a curmudgeon stuck in the muck and mire of your generation; your pride will let you down!! Within the first two weeks you should set up accounts and profiles on, at least, the following websites:

- **Facebook.com:** If you currently have a profile, create a business page. If you don't have a profile, create one and then create a business page. Don't create a fake profile just because you don't want people to identify you – yes, I personally know agents that have done this and no, it doesn't make any sense. Facebook does not like fake profiles and they will kick you out. If you are unsure how to set up a profile, talk with a pre-teen or teenager. Facebook has become the biggest party around. There are millions of users and millions of potential customers and if you don't think they're checking to see if you are on Facebook and other social websites, you'd be wrong; especially millenials. If you don't think they're talking about you (positively and negatively) you'd be wrong there too but by being a member of Facebook and other social media websites, you now have the opportunity to defend yourself by posting your side of the story. Keep in mind though that just as with any party there are rules of engagement:

- You wouldn't walk into a party and start ranting about how much you hate _____ (fill in the blank). This would not endear yourself to your fellow guests. Treat Facebook like you would any party you've been invited to. If you would like to have a private conversation with someone you can do that but be careful what you say and who you say it to.

- You certainly wouldn't start sharing those intimate or inappropriate photos of yourself and/or others by passing them out to everyone at the party (at least I hope you wouldn't); be careful how you post your photos on Facebook.

- Surely you wouldn't share a risqué photo or video of someone else who was not at a party and unable to defend himself. Don't do it on Facebook.

- Just as you wouldn't spend the entire party talking about what you do for a living, most of your posts from your personal profile should be personal and only occasionally should you share work related posts. If all you talk about is your work, your Facebook friends will begin blocking your posts the same as they would slowly back away from you at a face-to-face party. In general

72

80% of your conversation should be personal and 20% should be business.

- However, from your business page, you can flip-flop that and make it 80% business and 20% personal. So what business should you talk about? Certainly you will want to share the state of the market, any listings you have and your opinion of the market and just as importantly, ask questions just as you would at a face to face party. It is important to get to know your guests (those who "like" your business page and follow your posts.) By asking questions you also discover the issues your potential customers are facing. In Chapter 5 we talk about discovering the issues your potential clients are concerned with. Facebook is an inexpensive (read free) and effective way to post your questions.

- You can advertise your business on Facebook and the cost is minimal and you can track your advertisement's success rate. I encourage you to review Facebook's advertising offerings.

Zillow.com: Create an account and a profile. This is the most talked about and used website for buyers and sellers. It is critical that you have a presence on this site. Zillow rewards points for your participation on their site and the more points you accumulate the more times your name and profile appear when buyers and sellers perform searches. And, of course, you can purchase advertising and even zip code areas.

Trulia.com: Just as with Zillow.com this is a very popular site for buyers and sellers. Establish an account and a profile and become active in the community.

Linkedin.com: Ok, I admit I am not a Linkedin fan. Originally, it was supposed to be a Facebook environment for business people and you were to link to those you recommended and those who recommended you but I regularly get requests to link to someone just because they are a Realtor – as if that is reason enough to refer them. In my opinion Linkedin has somewhat lost its way as a useful website but you should still have a presence there and a complete profile. Use this site properly though by only linking to people you would recommend to others.

- **Google.com:** Google is the 800 pound Gorilla at the internet party. Other than Facebook, they rule the internet. Get familiar with the following:
  - *Google Analytics:* (Google it ☺) This tool helps give you insight into your website traffic and marketing effectiveness. It helps you write more effective ads and improve your SEO (Search Engine Optimization) for your website.

  - *Google Maps:* Map your company and yourself, and/or share places that matter to you. You and others can also write reviews about local businesses, towns or other places you've visited.

  - *Google Earth:* A must-have program you need to install on your computer. You can literally get a close up satellite view and street view of all the homes you plan to show your buyer. If you mail prospective listings to that out of town buyer prior to them coming to town, it is a very good bet that they will Google Earth these homes. If they see the four lane highway just up the street from the home that the listing agent failed to mention, they will wonder why you felt that home was a good candidate. Always review Google Earth before listing appointments and before sharing the listing with your prospective buyers.

  - *Gomo:* a Google based site that displays how your website will look on a smartphone. Use of smartphones to search the web is growing exponentially so if your website does not display correctly... well, I'm sure you understand the consequences of someone not being able to properly view your website on their smartphone.

YouTube.com: Excerpted from *10 fascinating YouTube facts that may surprise you (Feb 19, 2011 by Amy-Mae Elliot)* *http://mashable.com/2011/02/19/youtube-facts/* Direct comments are in quotes.

> "More video content is uploaded to YouTube in a 60 day period than the three major U.S. television networks created in 60 years! The average YouTube user spends between 15 and 25 minutes a day on the site."

As of February 2011:
– "YouTube had 490 million unique users worldwide per month that racked up an estimated 92 billion page views each month."
– "We spent around 2.9 billion hours on YouTube in a month."
– "There were over 150 years worth of YouTube videos watched every single day. So in other words, you could spend your life and your children's - children's lives watching YouTube." (a gargantuan waste of all of those lives indeed).
– "The most watched video, viewed by 282,151,886 users (and as of this writing an additional 100,000,000 had tuned in) was "Charlie bit my Finger".

Now if over 382 million viewers have watched one small child bite another small child's finger, I'm quite certain some of them will watch you introduce yourself as a Realtor and they might just want to contact you. To prove my point, I posted a video on YouTube while testing its linkage with Facebook. I had no intention of leaving the video on YouTube and I took it down after just three days but before I removed it I had 20 views and five comments on Facebook. Trust me, YouTube viewers will watch anything.

With YouTube, you now have the ability to reach a worldwide audience at almost no cost with the added bonus of creating your own "Channel". While it cost Oprah Winfrey millions if not billions of dollars to create her OWN channel, you can create one on YouTube for free and post all your housing related videos there. Further, you can point people to your channel who are following you on Twitter and/or Facebook. As an added bonus, you can view *YouTube Charts* to see continually updated information about what is popular on YouTube thus allowing you to tweak your videos and video descriptions for maximum viewing.

There are many other sites out there that can enhance your business. This book is not designed to teach you about all of them. Further, by the time you read this book it is possible, if not likely, that some of the internet websites mentioned will be obsolete or completely different. If you are not comfortable with a computer, take a class. If you aren't comfortable with the internet and all its trappings, read a book, take a class or view on-line tutorials. Better yet, ask your kids or grand-kids.

Trail Log:

Chapter 8: Understanding the local fauna OR getting to know the people.

No serious hiker goes off into the woods without a thorough understanding of the animals they may encounter along the way. The fauna of the woods are the buyers and sellers and it is important we understand them. What makes them attack? What causes them to run away? What foods do they prefer? And how should we talk to them?

In this chapter we'll explore techniques to discover your clients' wants and needs. We will discuss how you can establish your credibility and discover the various styles of communication techniques you can use to talk to the animals.

Just as you wouldn't wander up to all manner of sleeping animals and poke them just to learn how they react, at least I hope you wouldn't or your poking days may indeed be very short lived, you can't create marketing and advertising material until you know who your ideal client is. Have you ever used a shopping cart that has an agent's advertisement splayed across the top basket? *"Use me for all your housing needs!"* it pleads. Why? Why should said shopper use that agent as opposed to the other 10 agents she saw advertising the same way earlier in the day? What has that agent told her that would entice her to utilize their services? In fact, do they even know what her housing needs are? In all honesty, why should she help that agent when she doesn't know them and they've done nothing but exhorted her to use them for "all" her housing needs? A bit of a waste of perfectly good advertising dollars in my opinion; so what should you advertise? Read on...

Discovering the issues your potential clients fear
Spend a few minutes thinking about your ideal client and then ask yourself, what are they worried about? If you were one of them, what concerns would you have? The answer to this question is what you market. For example: You know to go to a dentist to fix your cavity because that is what dentists advertise. But if you've never used a dentist or you're new to town, which dentist should you use – after all, they all

advertise that they fix cavities? Of course you will most likely ask your circle of influence (we'll discuss using your circle of influence to help grow your business later) but if you're new to town you may not know who to ask. You may thumb through the Yellow pages or more likely Google local dentists. But if you are deathly afraid of dentists you will quickly narrow your search to those who specialize in sedation dentistry or dentists who specialize in this field in other ways. In other words, you will look for one who advertises a solution to your problem.

Our industry is no different. Buyers and sellers have a problem and they need it solved. You cannot solve every real estate issue because the industry is simply too broad; so you have to choose. Who do you like to work with and why? Ask yourself what problems you feel they have and create a solution for them.

Where you market, is also determined by who your potential customers/clients are but remember you don't need to spend oodles of money on marketing; just go to where these people are. Here's a concern I'll bet you have... *"I can't get clients because I don't have credibility and I can't get credibility because I don't have clients..."* Sound familiar?

This is not a chicken or egg issue. Credibility ALWAYS comes first. Remember people do business with you because:

1. They like you.
2. They trust you.
3. They believe you have their best interests in mind.
4. They believe you have market/industry knowledge. (i.e. credibility)

Certainly you're likable and you're trustworthy and you probably wouldn't be doing this if you didn't put other peoples' needs first so how do you get credibility?

Establishing creditability in three steps

1. Identify the niche market you want (as we discussed above).

2. Ask them what their concerns are. I could expand on this but the easiest way to ask them is too... well, just ask them. Whether in person, by phone, short seminars, Facebook, email... just ask, they'll tell you.

3. Answer those concerns through blogging, E-newsletters, seminars, one-on-one conversations, networking groups, tweets, etc...

How do you find the answers to their concerns? The internet of course!! *"Google it and ye shall know!"* Or if you prefer, read a book or ask a service provider. Remember, you don't have to be the source of all the information, simply be the source of the source so you can help others resolve their problem. Answer your niche market's concerns and worries and you'll develop credibility.

Understanding the local fauna OR when to approach and when to run

As a Realtor you will encounter every kind of animal out there and you may even discover a new species. Buyers and sellers come in all varieties with some that defy categorization, but in general we can lump them into a few categories to help us learn their communication styles...

Categorizing communication styles

(Courtesy of the National Association of Realtors, their comments are in quotes.)

This author's comments are, *italicized* and indented.

Think-They-Know-It-All:

"How to identify them: You tell the sellers that their house should be listed at the price you've identified, but these clients know better than

80

you. In fact, they know everything — at least they think they do. These clients' know-it-all attitude has their ego front and center.

How to deal with them: Ask a lot of questions about what they say. *'What will happen is they will quickly hit bottom,'* Brinkman says. *'They don't have depth to their knowledge.'* So, the best thing you can do is take a curious attitude and ask more and more specific questions until they start making big generalizations. Eventually, they'll realize they don't know as much as they're professing.

However, be careful not to step on their ego. You want to derail bad ideas, not embarrass them. So, for example, refer to documentation in a nonthreatening way (e.g., *'Have you seen this article?'*) to make your point."

> *I agree these folks do exist and their knowledge is often shallow but you would be wise to realize that they may be much more knowledgeable of the marketplace than you realize. Just because they don't have their facts and figures in front of them doesn't mean they haven't done thorough research. Tread cautiously ask questions that not only validate them but gently probe (for example: "You make an excellent point Mr. Seller, would you mind sharing with me where your information source was?") The answer can be very telling...*

The Yes Person

"How to identify them: These customers are highly agreeable but slow to deliver. Their people-pleasing tendency may get in the way of providing you with honest, valuable feedback to move forward in a transaction.

How to deal with them: Make it safe for these customers to be honest with you and show them there will be no relationship consequence if they say something negative. For example, say, *'If none of these houses work for you, Mr. Buyer, it's totally OK to tell me.'*

You'll need to make guesses at what they're thinking so you can then provide such reassurance to them that it's safe to provide honest feedback. By doing so, you'll actually create a customer for life — they'll perceive you as being sensitive to their feelings, Brinkman says."

> *I have lived in the Charlotte area since 1979. Over the years I have observed a very interesting phenomenon. No matter where someone is from, after they have lived here for a period of time they lose the ability to say "no". It's as if the southern air causes them to talk all around the subject, create false hope, give wishy-washy answers but never actually say no. They may even go so far as to not return phone calls or answer emails because they don't want to say no. If you find yourself with such a creature, get them comfortable with saying no by starting with small things and see how they respond. Of course the best way to find out is to simply ask them, "Mr. Buyer, are you trying to tell me you do not like this home? If so, what items would you like to see improved or changed?" Then again, there are those that can't wait to say "no"...*

The No Person
"How to identify them: They're discouraging and pessimistic. They'll probably find something wrong with every house you show them or any idea you present for selling their house.

How to deal with them: Break them out of their negativity. Take out a piece of paper, draw a line in the center, and ask them to list positives on one side and negatives on the other about the house they're viewing. Ask for the negatives first, since that's more on their mind, Brinkman notes. Once they've exhausted the negatives, refocus their attention to list a few positives.

Remember, the No Person tends to zoom in only on negatives — so a No Person who sees three things wrong with a home thinks everything is wrong with it and will be unable to focus on any positives. The paper-pen method will help you to refocus the No Person's attention on finding something positive. Plus, after a few homes, you'll be able to develop a list of criteria to show deal-breakers and what the client really desires in a home."

Our parents or grandparents would have called these people "grumpy old men (or women)". They are, in part, itching for a fight. If you find yourself working with someone who focuses on the negative be blunt. Say something to this affect:

"Mr. Buyer, no home is perfect and no home will fit your needs perfectly. Do you believe or can you see yourself (depending on if they are thinkers or feelers) purchasing a home that meets your most important needs? If so, let's be sure we identify and focus on those items. Is that ok with you?"

By the way, you can take advantage of the No Person by asking questions that give you the answer you want when they say "no". For example, "You wouldn't mind if I called on you tomorrow would you?" If they are inclined to say no as their first response, they've just agreed to let you call on them tomorrow. In other words, just as with math, two negatives multiplied together equal a positive.

The Nothing Person

"How to identify them: They tell you nothing, providing no feedback, verbal or nonverbal. You may grind to a halt with a Nothing Person because "I don't know" is often the first response to practically anything you ask.

How to deal with them: Try to guess at how they feel in a situation and offer statements to pry something out of them. Using the paper-pen method suggested above, you'll likely need to guess the pros and cons to put on the lists about the houses rather than rely on them telling you (e.g., *'This home has the open floor plan with the kitchen and living room. I'm guessing that's a positive for you, right?'*). They'll be more apt to provide you with feedback on whether your guess is right or wrong. Don't worry about guessing wrong — the aim is to get them to open up and externalize their thought process, Brinkman says."

Although I agree with these comments I believe it is critical that you ask permission to "guess" what they are thinking. No one likes others to put words in their mouth or to assume what they are thinking. First ask, "Mrs. Buyer would you mind if I shared with you what I believe are positive aspects of this house?"

As a side note, instead of asking the Nothing person what you believe they are thinking ask them instead how they feel. If they are not analytical they may appear to be wishy-washy and a Nothing Person, but it might just be that you are not asking the right question in the right way. If you encounter a buyer who is not providing you with positive or negative feedback ask questions that elicit emotion instead (for example: instead of asking "what do you think of this living room?" ask "How do you feel when you're in this living room?" or "How do you see yourself using this room?")

We don't all think the same way and (no pun intended) we don't all think. Many people make decisions based upon their feelings and gut instincts. Steve Jobs (founder and CEO of Apple) created a highly successful corporation because he wanted computers to be user-friendly and have a different look and feel (which is why the first MAC's had a white background so they would feel more like paper

84

*rather than a computer). Hundreds, if not thousands
of successful people feel their way to success.*

*If you're not getting the response you want, change
your question and change your paradigm of how
people make decisions.*

The Tank

"How to identify them: They are pushy, ruthless, and loud. They rant
when something upsets them. They demand action. For example, *'How
dare you suggest listing my house for such a low price? You have no clue
what you're talking about!'*

How to deal with them: Give the Tank 60 seconds to vent, no more and
no less. If you allow a Tank to go longer, the verbal attack will escalate
and it'll be difficult to refocus. So after the 60-second tirade, interrupt
using your client's name and highlight some of the rant to show you
were listening and reassure that you're on the same side (e.g. *'John,
John. We both care about getting the most for your property. I heard you
say ... '*)

Then, repeat three of the statements you heard, Brinkman says. Why
three? Brinkman, a naturopathic physician, calls it the generalization
point, in which after repeating three statements back to a person that
recounts what the customer said that person then subconsciously truly
feels heard.

After you playback what they said, offer your bottom-line solution, but
make your solution direct and to the point. Tanks appreciate
assertiveness."

*Validating a Tank's comment is crucial because they
need to believe you have heard and understand their
concern. Often we use assertiveness and
aggressiveness interchangeably. Be careful that you
understand the difference between assertiveness and
aggressiveness. To be assertive is to be positive and*

*confident; whereas to be aggressive means to be
hostile and quarrelsome. Guess which one the Tank
would **love** for you to be? Don't be aggressive.*

*I believe Tanks are playing a domination game.
They are the wild boar looking to dominate the fight.
You can roll over and let them win, you can walk
away, or you can puff up, stand your ground and
assertively protect your position. Tanks often
become your greatest and most loyal advocate if you
stand your ground and prove to them you are their
equal.*

*If you don't feel you have the fight in you, let them
know you don't have the time, inclination or desire
to wrestle with them and walk away. Many years
ago I was itching for a fight – over what I have no
idea – when I confronted my wife, she smiled and
lovingly said, "I choose not to participate" and
walked away. Well that took all the air out of my
sails and there I sat dead in the water. Walking
away can be just as effective as standing your
ground but you must be as confident as my wife and
you must be sure the Tank understands you are not
running away, in which they win, you are choosing
to walk away, in which they lose.*

The Grenade

"How to identify them: You'll feel like you want to take cover. The
Grenade provides unwarranted tantrums that seem disproportionate to the
circumstance. Unlike the Tank, who usually has a focused argument, the
Grenade surfaces as explosive rants on anything and everything.

How to deal with them: Don't give Grenades any time to vent: They feed
on their negative energy, and it'll only make them angrier. Immediately
raise your voice to interrupt, using their name (e.g. *'John, John. I care, I
care ... You don't have to feel this way. We're going to work this out.'*)

86

Don't tell them to calm down; you'll only make them more irate. Instead, you calm down: Take a breath and relax your tone, Brinkman suggests. Say: *'Let's take a moment and talk about it.'* You want to create a break in the conversation to allow them time to calm down so they'll be able to refocus on what their true concerns are."

Regarding Grenades, I must admit I don't entirely agree with Dr. Brinkman's advice. Telling a Grenade, "you don't have to feel this way" is essentially telling them how they are supposed to feel. How do you think they'll react? I have dealt with Grenades and they can come out of left field with concerns, worries, and complaints you could never have thought of and they can go off at the oddest times and at the oddest angles.

Personally I have found that by acknowledging their concerns as you go, they quickly run out of steam (for example: before the Grenade goes on to the next rant, clarify the first one… "I'm sorry for interrupting you but if I understand you correctly, you're concerned that closing has been moved 15 minutes is that correct?") Often when we hear our words parroted back to us we discover just how unwarranted or unreasonable they are. I do agree with Dr. Brinkman that staying calm is essential to defusing the situation (no pun intended). Grenades will make your blood boil because they go off at a moment's notice. Practice breathing exercises to keep yourself calm.

If you've had a troubled client in the past (or you have one now) jot down which category you think they fall in and make a few notes about how to handle them differently; because I can assure you if you've dealt with them once you will deal with them again…

_____

_____

_____

Ask an angry momma bear to do you a favor

In closing, if you are working with a client, customer or agent that you sense does not particularly like you, ask them to do you a small favor. Keep it small but start your sentence with, *"[name], would you do me a small favor and…?"* Now you might be wondering, why would they do me a favor if they don't like me? Exactly!! If your request is truly small (and it needs to be small) then they will be hard pressed to say no and if they don't say "no" then they must like you otherwise they wouldn't do a favor for you.

You are playing a little trick on their mind. You see, we have great discomfort when we hold two dissimilar thoughts at the same time. For example, it is hard to be a member of PETA (People for the Ethical Treatment of Animals) and at the same time wear fur coats or eat red meat. It is very discomforting to dislike someone AND do them a favor; one of those thoughts has to give. Psychologists refer to this phenomenon as cognitive dissonance but whatever you call it, the next time you sense someone doesn't like you, ask them to do you a very small favor and watch what happens.

Trail Log:

_____

_____

_____

_____

_____

_____

_____

_____

_____

_____

_____

_____

_____

_____

Chapter 9: Learning how to talk to the animals OR conflict resolution.

Before we discuss conflict resolution, now would be a good time to talk about how I believe people think...

How people think

In my opinion, there are two types of thinkers: Internal thinkers and external thinkers.

Internal thinkers (like my wife) sit quietly and absorb what you are saying to them, they process the information and then they respond.

External thinkers (like me) think by talking aloud to themselves or to someone else.

Now let's "think" about these two types trying to communicate. The external thinker (or the nervous real estate agent) keeps talking and talking while the internal thinker keeps absorbing and absorbing. The internal thinker is trying to process the spoken words but the information keeps coming because the external thinker keeps talking. When the external thinker is done he may become uncomfortable with the silence or he may have another thought and so he fills the void with even more information and the internal thinker has yet more information to process. As such, the internal thinker never gets a chance to process and respond.

If two external thinkers are communicating they may simply talk all over each other, neither one really processing the information.

Two internal thinkers can communicate well but only if they are willing to share their thoughts because they tend to be comfortable with the silence and are, in general, good listeners. Of course this could also result in a very boring evening of staring into one another's eyes (which may end up, on the other hand, not being so boring after all).

If you find the seller interrupting you, you probably have an external thinker. Let them talk. The more they talk, the more they'll debate and answer their own arguments. (ie. *"Why do you think we charge too much?"* Seller *"blah, blah, blah* {arguing for both sides and then concluding}, *well maybe it's not too much but it sure seems like it")*

Before talking with buyers and sellers consider how you think. If you are an external thinker you are going to have to train yourself to be comfortable in silence. If you are an internal thinker, you will need to learn to ask open-ended questions, particularly if your potential client is also an internal thinker; otherwise it will be two hours of you staring at each other. No matter how you think or they think, you must give them the opportunity to respond and share their thoughts.

What kind of thinker are you? _____

Calming the angry mama bear OR conflict resolution
Of course the conflicts we have with people are as varied as those people and the debated subject matter but in general when dealing with conflict resolution, you should practice the following:

- Know your audience
  - What is their communication style? (are they internal or external thinkers)
  - Understand their wants, their needs and desires, their concerns, and their issues.

- Empathize and acknowledge their concern. This is a critical step, even if (especially if) you believe their concern is trivial. Ponder, for a moment, the last time you had a customer complaint and you <u>felt</u> you weren't being heard or that your concern was not acknowledged. How did that make you <u>feel</u>? Everyone needs to feel their concern is legitimate no matter how silly or trivial others think it is. Did you notice that I underlined the word feel and felt? I did this to point out that our concerns and issues are often logical at their core but they are encased by our emotions. You cannot resolve the issue until you have dissolved the emotion that surrounds it. This is especially true if we think someone else's issue is trivial because while we're *thinking* it's trivial, they are *feeling* it is legitimate. In other words, it is the emotionally charged momma bear protecting her young VS the bear who is thinking, I'll put my money on the mama bear protecting her young every time.

To remove the emotional skin that surrounds the issue, try phrases that start with…

- *"I understand how you feel."* Of course only say this if you truly mean it, otherwise say something like…

- *"I'm sorry but I am having difficulty relating to how you are feeling but I certainly respect your right to it and I want to help resolve the problem."* We can't always understand how others feel but we can acknowledge their right to feel that way.

- *"If I understand you correctly you're saying…"* It can be very effective to restate their concern back to them. Often when we hear our own complaints from another person we realize that issue may not have the same import as we had originally given it. Or if they are reasonable we appreciate that the other person gets it.

- *"I agree, that is unreasonable and I would feel the same way if I were in your shoes. Let's see if we can work together to resolve the issue."* (Notice that I said "we" not "I" so that the seed is planted that I need their help to solve their issue.)

- *"That is a legitimate concern/problem and we need to address it."*

- Never dismiss the problem as trivial or not worth your attention. And never imply or state that they don't have a right to their issue. If you do, pack your things… You're toast.

- Solve their problem, not yours:
  - The reduction in commission may be the issue but if you can solve the seller's problem by helping them hold on to their equity, while you charge your desired commission, they'll be happy.

- In the end though, if you remember only one thing from this Chapter, remember this:
  - **If you do not ask permission to help solve the problem, you become the problem!!** (Do yourself a favor and slowly read this statement again.)

Boy have I learned this one the hard way. If you would like to test my reasoning, the next time your significant other starts to complain about something, don't ask permission to help solve the problem, simply say *"You know what you should do?"* then duck.

So how should you ask permission?
> *"May I offer a suggestion?"*
> *"If I understand you correctly you're saying _____, would you mind if I shared my thoughts on the matter?"*
>
> *"Would you mind if I shared what I have done in the past when presented with this problem?"*

How might you ask permission?

_____

_____

_____

If they say "no" then they don't want your help. Don't become disappointed or upset, there may not be a ready-answer or they already know what to do but they just want to blow off steam. Let them. They may be willing to ask for help later. If however, they are open to exploration, consider the following methods:

- Explore the issue:
    - Ask open-ended questions that help them explore the issue. These questions may help them solve their own problem. Open-ended questions begin with: what, how and why.
    - Ask closed ended questions to get a yes or no response thus creating buy-in.

        For example: *"I understand your concern to be _____. Please help me understand why this is a concern. What about _____ is troubling you? If we resolve _____ are you ready to move forward?"*)

        The response to this last question will more than likely be "yes", "no" or "I don't know". In any case their answer will help you move closer to resolving the issue because they will either be ready to move forward or you will understand that more exploration of the issue is required.

- The obstacle is not always the obstacle:
    - Often what, on the surface, appears to be the issue is simply a blanket that covers the real concern. For example, the commission we charge can be a point of contention during the listing presentation. If we do not explore the reasons behind the seller's hesitancy to pay the commission, we may never discover the real reason they do not want to pay that amount. In the past, the seller may have used a real estate agent that charged the same commission percentage we are proposing but that agent provided services that, in the eyes of the seller, were poor and did not justify the amount of commission charged. So we see that it is not, necessarily, the amount of commission that is at issue but the need for the seller to realize a return on their investment.

        Should you provide service above and beyond the seller's expectation, it is a very good bet the commission charged will become a non-issue. Asking open-ended questions will help you discover the real reason behind what appears to be the obstacle.

- You don't always have to resolve the issue before moving on:
  - I know, I said earlier that you must resolve their issue before moving on. But what if you can't? What if you don't have the answer or the time is not right? The delay tactic, as I refer to it, is one way to handle this situation. It can be effective because it kicks the can down the road. Don't get me wrong, I understand that unless the consumer completely forgets about their issue or it is resolved and/or dissolved along the way, that concern will have to be dealt with at some point. The delay tactic is used, though, to deal with the issue at a more appropriate or, shall I say, better prepared time. As with all things, there is a more proper time and place. Read on...

What to say...

"That is a great question, do you mind if we address that when we get to that part of the presentation?"

"Having just seen your home, I'm not prepared to answer that question and I wouldn't want to give you wrong information. Do you mind if we address that at our follow up meeting?" Now how cool was that, you deferred the issue, bought yourself some time and essentially scheduled your next meeting.

In teaching, this is referred to as the parking lot technique. The parking lot technique allows us to park students' questions until a more appropriate time, either written in the corner of the white board or on a piece of paper so that the student feels acknowledged and, if unanswered, the question can be dealt with later. The interesting thing is, I can't tell you the last time I had to address a question that was placed in the parking lot because it was either answered along the way or the student stopped caring about it. I've discovered that sometimes delaying the answer to a question actually answers the question.

- Are they complaining just to complain? Have you ever yelled at your spouse, significant other, children or pet only to realize they really hadn't done anything wrong? Were you just blowing off steam or itching for a fight because some other thing happened during the day that you had no control over?

— Listen and convey empathy (i.e. put yourself in their shoes) but don't try to solve the problem unless you ask permission or they ask for help.

— If you work with either withdrawn or expired seller's (the listing, not the seller), you will most likely experience sellers looking to vent. They are frustrated and they may recognize that their unwillingness or inability to reduce their price was, in fact, the problem but it is difficult for them to admit it and they are angry with themselves for being in the situation they are in. They are looking to vent and you are a convenient set of ears. Let them vent and practice the if/then closing technique (more on this later).

Thick skin, broad shoulders, and an even temper are your best friends when it comes to conflict resolution, but just as importantly remember that if you do not ask permission to help solve the problem, you become the problem!

Trail Log:

Chapter 10: Locating the local fauna OR prospecting for sellers.

Searching for the local fauna

Several years ago a large real estate company in Kansas City surveyed their agents to find out where they were getting their listings. To participate in the study, the agent had to have closed at least $2 million in sales volume or 20 sales in the first 12 months they were in business. Here is what they found:

What was your main source for buyers: (from best source to worst source)

1. Personal acquaintances

2. Floor duty

3. Open houses

4. Social groups

5. Networking

6. Cold calling

7. Model homes

8. Expireds

What was your main source for sellers? (From best source to worst source)

1. Friends and relatives

2. Social farming

3. Open houses

4. Floor duty

5. FSBO's

6. Expireds

7. Door-to-door and talking to neighbors

What the study did not discuss is the quantity of buyers/sellers from each category. But I am willing to make a large bet that the vast majority of these first year agents' client base came from the first category – friends and family. See a more recent study done in 2011 below.

This study was also done before the internet really influenced real estate. So I would also wager heavily that Social Groups and Networking would now be rated higher and they would be centered on Facebook, Zillow, Trulia and other Social Media websites. The fundamental need to network and connect with others has not changed. How we go about networking may be changing but the need for it will never change. Get out there and mingle every day; it is the most important thing you will do to grow your business. It is the fertilizer, if you will, for the tree you are trying to grow or as we like to say in this business, *"This ain't the CIA."* Secret agents fail every time in this business.

I know I sound like a broken record, but you can break records (groan if you must but this pun was intended) if you will strongly focus on your circle of influence and regularly let them know you are a real estate agent looking for buyers and sellers.

2011 study:
> On 6/29/2011 a study was done asking 16 – 34 year olds where they decide to go to dinner, movies etc… 69% said they ask friends and family before deciding what movie to see or place to eat. 69%!! Now I know 16 year olds aren't buying homes but 34 year olds are. If they ask their friends and family where to eat, I can assure you they'll ask them who they should work with to buy or sell a home.

↑ **Talk to your friends and family! It is the most important prospecting you will do!!**

> As I write this, I may have heard you say, *"I just moved here and I don't have any friends and family. What am I supposed to do*

98

now?" I understand. When I entered the business of real estate I did not call on my friends and family. Was it a mistake? In retrospect I don't think I gave my relationships enough credit, so yes, I think it was a mistake. You may have more friends and family than you realize (of course if you have more family than you realize you may want to look into that). Do not let the lack of a circle of influence prevent your success.

In fact, your circle of influence may be larger than you think. If you're new to the area, you have (or will have) made contact with dentists, doctors, and other service providers, local grocers, delivery services, and yes, coffee shops too. You've dined at restaurants, shopped at local retail stores and maybe had your car repaired. And even if you don't have family here, they're somewhere, and the odds are they know people looking to move to your market. Work the exercises in this book to examine and expand your circle of influence.

If you have a circle of influence but you don't think they'll support you, try them and if they still don't or won't support you then brush them off and develop a new circle. Never let others, or the lack thereof, define your success!

Working with "moose and squirrel" OR tapping the expired and withdrawn market

The aforementioned study conducted by that large Kansas City real estate firm was done back in 2002 when the national real estate market was healthy and growing and therefore the number of expired and withdrawn listings was expectedly lower on the list. Today expired and withdrawn listings can be a reasonable listing source, but you will most likely have to be flexible on the commission you charge because these sellers may have little equity and thus little room to reduce their price to be more competitive. You will also need to be very empathetic of their frustration and their situation, but at the same time, very assertive in making it known that it was most likely the price, the condition and/or the location of the home that was the source of their woes. The seller

99

will, in all likelihood, blame the previous agent for their woes. Certainly that agent may have been a contributing factor, but it is much more likely the failure to sell can be traced to the home's condition, price and/or location. Do not jump on the seller's bandwagon and join them in beating up the previous agent. Stay focused on what now needs to happen to sell the home.

To acquire these listings, you must contact them in a variety of ways quickly, repeatedly and frequently because if they are going to re-list they will, in all likelihood, do it quickly. With this said, be mindful of the National Do-Not Call list. The fines are hefty.

So how do you market to them? Of course if they aren't on the Do-Not-Call list then call them. Also drive by the home and drop off relevant information (neighborhood sales statistics, comparable sales information, general market conditions, etc…). If you're comfortable, knock on the door. Be courteous and honest with your intentions. Be prepared with your usual seller folder but be sure to include recent sales information and active listings so the would-be seller understands the current market. It is very possible, if not likely, that the seller has had no updates on current market conditions from their former agent. I say this because in working this market in the past I have contacted sellers who did not even know their home had expired because their agent never contacted them about the pending expiration date nor about renewing the listing. If the agent doesn't even tell the seller their listing is about to expire, it is a pretty good bet they aren't telling them about the current state of the market.

You must act quickly with these sellers. They may have already decided who they will hire (often while they are still listed with the former agent). So if you decide to work in this market have all of your marketing material ready to go. Further, you must contact them a minimum of six times. Interestingly, many expired and withdrawn listings do relist, but they do so only after being contacted by the same agent at least six times. Of course the vast majority of agents give up after three or four tries so there remains a large pool of expired and withdrawn listings for a relatively small pool of real estate agents willing to persevere.

Many firms will have "Expired and Withdrawn" documents and marketing material. Even if they don't, the content isn't as critical as the contact... In other words it isn't terribly critical what you say, so long as you say it a minimum of six times. It is very much like dating. The seller feels as if they have been jilted and they want to know if your intentions are serious or you're just along for the ride.

Trying to catch the shy field mouse OR marketing to For Sale By Owners (FSBO)

Working this market is very similar to working the expired/withdrawn market. The only difference is you have more time because the FSBO is not immediately interested in listing with any firm. The key to working this area of the business is to be truthful and honest. Of course this should always be true but it is especially true with FSBO's. They want the unvarnished truth because they are an inherently untrusting group for many reasons and their reasons run from poor service from a past real estate agent to a general distrust of the entire real estate industry.

Should you phone a FSBO do not use the tired line about having a buyer interested in their home, even though you know it's not true, just so you can set up a meeting. Also be sure the FSBO is not on the Do-Not-Call list. Remember, just because their phone number is on the sign that does not give you the right to call them to solicit their business. If they are on the Do-Not-Call list you may only contact them via telephone if you have a legitimate buyer.

I have worked this market on several occasions. Although I have not always gotten the listing I have always received an invitation to visit with the seller using the following script:

"Mrs. Seller, thank you for taking my call. I understand you are cooperating with brokers. In other words, if I had a buyer interested in your home and I assisted in the sale, you would be willing to pay a buyer agent commission is that correct? I will be honest with you Mrs. Seller, I

don't know whether I have a buyer or not until I see what features your home has to offer. Would you mind if I stopped by to tour your home?"

There are a couple of statements in this script I would like to expand on. Often times FSBO's will indicate on their sign that they will "co-broke" – thus the statement *"I understand you are cooperating with brokers..."* If it is not clear that they will co-broke then I modify the script to say something like *"If I had a buyer that was interested in purchasing your home, would you be willing to pay a buyer agent fee?"* My second thought goes to the honesty of the script - I truly do not know if I have a buyer interested in their house. By being honest with the seller I have found they are very open to meeting with me.

Prior to your first meeting I suggest you compile a FSBO package to give to the seller. In it, be sure to include the NC Residential Property Disclosure Form and explain that the law requires all sellers to complete the form. Many, if not most, FSBOs do not know they have to complete this form.

As with withdrawn and expired listings, you will need to follow up a minimum of six times. The good news is you will not need to work with the same sense of urgency and your six contacts can be spread out over a few weeks. Most FSBO's will grow weary of marketing their home, no-show buyers and the roller coaster ride of excitement and disappointment resulting from buyers' interests waxing and waning. Again, have a FSBO marketing plan ready to go so you can maximize the efficiency of working this market. And remember, it is not terribly important what you say, so long as you say it a minimum of six times.

Open houses

"Ugh!" That is my first thought when I think about hosting an open house. Do they work? It depends on what you are trying to accomplish. I have gotten a lot of paperwork done while sitting in a lightly visited open house. On the other hand, I have had opportunities to meet the neighbors and an occasional "looky loo" and even an actual buyer on occasion. Even with these frustrations, I would not entirely dismiss open houses.

There are markets where hosting an open house can be very productive and other markets that will assure you will be able to read and reply to all your unopened emails because visitors will be far and few between. I have never sold the home at which the open house was being held and I have never met an agent who has – that is not to say it hasn't happened. I believe early in your career you should host open houses if only for the practice of meeting and greeting and talking to people about buying and selling homes. You will get at least a neighbor or two and that creates the opportunity to practice your various presentations and elevator speeches. I also think, and I am not being facetious, it is a good opportunity to complete all of that busy work that has been building up while you wait for the occasional walk-in. Speaking of waiting, do not close the open house early just because no one has shown up, I cannot tell you why this occurs but it is not uncommon to have a flurry of activity moments before your open house is scheduled to end.

When should you host an open house? Traditionally it is on weekends during the day but I have visited evening open houses and they can be very effective. Study the property to determine under what conditions it shows best. Also consider working with other agents in your office or even other companies to coordinate multiple open houses in the same neighborhood. Oh and just as you probably shouldn't go hiking alone in a forest you are unfamiliar with, you should always take a hiking buddy with you to your open house; a spouse, boy (or girl) friend, or a teenager will work nicely. It is very important that you have a second set of eyes monitoring not only the house but the visitors who may frequent it. I strongly encourage you to never host an open house by yourself.

In closing our open house discussion (groan if you must but that's funny), you must put directional signs out, or you will be guaranteed a long and lonely afternoon, but be mindful of the county and/or city and HOA sign ordinances. Also, if you check on the Listing Agreement that you will host an open house, you must do it or you are in breach of your fiduciary duties and contractual obligations to the seller. If you feel you can't bring yourself to conduct an open house, do not check that you will.

Whether you are talking with a guest at an open house or a withdrawn or expired listing, or general public about their housing needs, do not engage in first substantial contact until you have presented the Working with Real Estate Agents Brochure.

Warning dangerous trail ahead OR an important discussion about the Working with Real Estate Agents Brochure

Many agents continue to struggle with disclosing and discussing the Working with Real Estate Agents Brochure at first substantial contact. Year after year complaints pour into the NC RE Commission because agents fail to present the brochure; it is not an optional part of your agent duties, it is a requirement.

If you fail to present the brochure and the consumer files a complaint with the NC RE Commission (which based on recent history is not out of the realm of possibility), you will have a very long and lonely ride to Raleigh. And if your BIC rides with you, it will be an even longer ride you could only hope would be a tad lonelier. Please present the brochure in all real estate sales transactions and remember the NC RE Commission requires that you:

1. Present the brochure.
2. Review the contents of the brochure.
3. Decide the type of agency relationship, if any, you will have with the consumer.
4. Discuss how you will be compensated.
   And you are to do all of this at first substantial contact.

First substantial contact arises in the following ways:
- The consumer begins talking about their housing wants, needs and desires.
- They share confidential information.
- They share motivational information.
- They share their willingness to accept terms and conditions of a potential contract.
- OR YOU ASK ABOUT ANY OF THE ABOVE.

104

- Lastly, even if none of the above occurs because you are meeting a buyer at a listing for the first time (a clear risk to your safety), you must present and review the brochure before opening the door to the home.

The review of the brochure does not have to be intimidating or awkward. I encourage you to practice it regularly so you can recite its contents even if you don't have a copy with you. To adequately explain the brochure you need only remember four things:

1. Your fiduciary duties (LOADS)
   - Loyalty: Put your client's interests ahead of your own while keeping confidential information confidential. Only material facts are to be shared with others.
   - Obedience: Obey your client's lawful instructions.
   - Accountability: You are accountable for the safety of their property and their monies.
   - Disclosure: You must disclose all information to your clients but only material facts to a customer.
   - Skill, Care and Diligence: You are expected to use reasonable skill, care and diligence in protecting your client's interests and revealing all material facts to all parties.

2. You and your firm's responsibilities as dual agents.
3. Your responsibilities as a designated agent.
4. If the buyer refuses to hire you, your obligation to warn them of the italicized text at the bottom of the brochure's flap. In essence it is the buyer's Miranda warning.

When talking with sellers, it is rather obvious that the brochure needs to be discussed, but I sometimes find it difficult to discover when first substantial contact is about to occur when I'm talking to a potential buyer because they will blurt out confidential or motivational information seemingly from out of the blue. I have literally had to put up a timeout sign to stop someone from saying anything more before I've presented the contents of the brochure.

To address this, I now discuss the brochure's contents early in our conversation. I find it much easier to say right up front, *"Did you know that North Carolina allows agents to represent buyer's needs? Are you familiar with buyer agency in North Carolina?"* They can say *"yes"* or *"no"* or they could tell me they wrote the book on the subject. Regardless of their answer it is my way of entering into a discussion about the brochure. I have found that it is a very unobtrusive way to introduce and enter into a discussion about agency.

⚐ Present the Working with Real Estate Agents Brochure and discuss its contents. It is your ticket of admission to the big show!

Asking your fellow hikers where the best views are OR prospecting tips

Of course you have to have a potential prospect to present the brochure to. When asking others to help you find them remember, you don't have to be in their face to be "in their face". There are many ways to ask for business. Just be sure you're in touch with at least five members of your circle of influence every day. Take them to lunch (either dutch, they treat or you treat but don't treat every time or it will make them feel awkward and you'll go broke), share a cup of coffee, go for a walk, go shopping, visit someone who is sick, and take a meal with you (make it easy on them and put it in a disposable dish), if they do volunteer work, you do volunteer work with them. Do you get the idea? This is not dialing for dollars it is about spending time with people, taking an interest in them and showing them the value you bring to the relationship.

In most cases, they will ask, *"How's business?"* and with that, they have given you permission to talk about your growing or – maybe at the moment – stagnant business, so take advantage of it.

I often hear agents tell me that their BIC instructs them to always say, *"Business is great; it's a great time to buy or sell a home."* or words to that affect. Do we really think that our friends and family don't read the newspaper or watch the news? Be honest; let them know that business is hard (if it is) but that's why buyers and sellers should work with you because you have the tenacity and "stick-to-it-ness" to provide the outstanding service needed in today's market – after all even in a down market consumers buy and sell homes.

All elements of this business are important but I promise you if you will focus on friends, family and your other circle of influence contacts before spending money on advertising to the masses, you will work half as hard and be twice as successful... Who wouldn't want that?

I know, I know, you just can't see yourself *saying, "So who do you know that's looking to buy or sell a home? What is their name? Can I use you as a referral? Would you call them on my behalf?"* I don't like saying those things either. So if you'd like something else to say to your friends and family, how about these statements...

Ask them, *"So how is your business going?"* Most likely they'll reciprocate and ask how your business is going. (If they don't they'll ask eventually) and then say:

- *"I'm always looking for buyers and sellers. I love when I find someone that I can help!"* (Say this sincerely and smiling. Also, if possible, give them an example of how you recently helped a buyer or seller)

- *"I'm excited to be in a business where I can really help people with their major life decisions. I want to build my business on integrity and outstanding customer service. That seems to be missing in customer service today wouldn't you agree?"*

- *"Business is going well but as with all small business we need to continue to grow and I'm always on the lookout for new clients to help."* Your friends and family are no fools. They get what you're saying. Don't say anything more and see if they'll offer something up.

- *"There sure are a lot of agents out there. I don't know how buyers and sellers figure out which ones to use. I know for me, having a friend tell me about an agent they know would make my decision a lot safer and easier. Wouldn't you agree?"*

- *"May I ask you a question? If you were going to hire a contractor to do some work, what steps would you take?"*

- *"Hi (Name) this is (me) I'm making a business call. Do you have a couple of minutes?"* (If they don't have a couple of minutes, respect that and ask when you can call back. I really like to start the conversation this way because it sets the mood and allows me to become assertive in asking. If you do this, only spend two or three minutes on business then move on to asking them how they are doing. Overall though keep the conversation short.)

- My personal favorite, *"Joe, I respect your opinion, would you help me think of a few ways I can locate potential buyers and sellers?"* You've complimented Joe, you've planted the seed that he has good ideas and you've opened the door to ask if he knows anyone. And you have created a reason to follow up with him after you have tried his idea.

Diagnosing prospecting scripts
In general, all prospecting scripts can be broken down into these elements...

- **Why you are calling**... You can help people they know.

- **What they can do to help...** Help them help you by being specific as to who you're looking for. If they ask, *"who are you looking for?"* and you don't have an answer, it makes it hard for them to help you. Think about who you are looking for and write it down. I understand that at this point you will take anybody but you can probably narrow it down somewhat (think about price range, buying/selling time frame, residential VS Commercial, foreclosures, etc...)

I speak with a lot of people and it is not uncommon for someone to tell me their spouse has lost a job. I often offer to assist them if they'll send me a resume or if they tell me what kind of work their spouse is looking for. One of two things usually happens. Either they never send the resume or they tell me what their spouse used to do but not, necessarily, what they want to do or are willing to do. It makes it difficult to help them if I don't know how to help them.

- **How they can help you...** Teach them how they can help you find potential clients by saying something like, *"What I've found is that the people I can help the most are..."*

- **Why they should help you...** 10 second elevator speech or two or three reasons their referrals should work with you.

- **Where we go from here...** End all calls with a statement that you will follow up or talk with them soon. They have to know that they can expect to have a conversation with you in the near future; after all, they may be holding the name of a referral until the next time you call.

The purpose of the prospect phone call

They've provided you with a prospect's name. Now what? Well now it's time to call the prospect. And I mean call them now! One of the biggest mistakes I see agents make is getting the opportunity to contact a prospective client and then not doing it or not doing it in a timely matter. Why don't they call? Who knows – fear, lack of confidence, the list is endless. Several years ago I gave a new agent the opportunity to contact a friend of mine who wanted to list several pieces of raw land. I did not sell raw land but I told my friend I would have an agent call him. I had taken a liking to this new agent and I thought he would appreciate the opportunity (wouldn't you?). Two weeks after I gave this new agent my friend's contact information I asked how the phone call went. The new agent said that he had not called him. Two weeks!! Not only did he not get the listing but he embarrassed me because I told my friend someone

109

would call him and they didn't. You must make the phone call. I can all but guarantee that if you do not call them, you will not receive another referral from your source again.

When contacting prospective clients, remember that the purpose of the phone call is to set up the face-to-face meeting. You are not trying to close the deal on the phone. In other words, don't try to get the listing on the phone, simply get the listing appointment. Getting the appointment is your primary objective so keep the conversation coming back to this point. Give the prospect two broad choices and keep narrowing those choices until you've got an appointment set up.

Let's look at an example where we are at the point of attempting to set up the face-to-face meeting:

☎ *"I think that is a great question and I'd like to sit down and talk with you further about that. Would earlier in the week or later in the week work for you?"*

☎ *"Early, ok Monday or Tuesday? Tuesday it is."*

☎ *"Would the morning or afternoon work better? Great, Tuesday morning it is."*

☎ *"Would 9 AM or 10 AM work better for you? Terrific, I'll see you Tuesday morning at 10 AM. May I have your cell phone number in case I'm running late?"*

Often adults will answer the question asked. Whether that habit comes from our public schools and the traditional classroom environment or not, adults will typically answer a question asked before thinking about the consequences of their answer. Ask someone their name or where they're from and they'll usually answer it before thinking about why you need to know. With this in mind, ask your question and you'll more than likely get an answer.

In the above dialogue did you notice that we asked for their cell phone number in case *"we are running late"*? Primarily we want their cell phone number so we can follow up with them to assure that they will show up at the appointment. If you are unsure the prospect will meet you, on the day of your meeting, try this:

☎ *"Hi George [assuming, of course, George is in fact their name.], this is _____ I just wanted to let you know I'm planning to be on time and I am on my way , but traffic is a little heavy so I may be running a few minutes late. I apologize but I just wanted to let you know that I should be there no later than ____ O'clock."*

The primary purpose of this phone call is to remind the prospect that you will be at the appointed place and you expect to see them there too. You may also want to mention the referral source's name as a way to publicly commit this referral lead to attend the meeting... As in *"[referral source] mentioned that you [name an activity]. I'm looking forward to hearing more about that."*

Be sure to follow up with your referral source. Alert them as to the time and place of the meeting and then follow up with them after the meeting to let them know how it went. Whether you get the opportunity to meet with the referral or not or whether you were able to assist them in the purchase or sale of a property or not, be sure to reward your source for the act of giving you a referral, not for the outcome. Remember too that you may only give gifts of nominal value. Often times a hand written thank you note is more than enough to stimulate additional referrals; your source merely wants to know that their efforts have not gone unnoticed and have been appreciated.

Trail Log:

Chapter 11: Learning the call of the wild OR what to say to sellers and how to list property.

Before talking about listing properties and what to say to the sellers to make that happen, let's take a moment and discuss properties one should not list. To be perfectly frank, not every house is worth listing. Having a sign in the yard is not why you got into this business. Selling the house with the sign in the yard, now we're talking.

Reasons to take a listing:
- You might pick up a buyer.
- You'll get opportunities to talk with people and further your craft.
- You'll have reasons to talk with your friends and family and show them you are moving your business forward.
- It is fun pushing a sign in the yard and admiring it as if you planted the flag at the top of the Northern Terminus of the AT.
- You might, just might, sell it (assuming it will appraise).

But there are just as many reasons not to take a listing:
- The listing will grow stale and this may reflect poorly on you, reducing your chances of getting another listing in that neighborhood.

- Ill-will between the seller and you can quickly grow when a listing has little activity (i.e. no showings).

- You choose to list your best friend or family member's house knowing that it is overpriced or in poor condition with little chance to sell. This can be very damaging to your ability to get referrals from them and other friends and family members because the odds are they will talk to each other. If you don't feel good about listing their house, in my opinion, it is better to refer them to another agent.

If you do refer the transaction out to another agent, should you request a referral fee from that agent? I suppose that depends on how close you are to the prospective seller and how you think they would react if they find out about your referral fee during the transaction or at the closing table. Do not assume, however, that they will be just "peachy keen" with you receiving a referral fee, especially if you don't tell them.

- Over-priced houses do not produce quality buyers. In fact they rarely produce buyers at all. Even if you find that "sucker born every minute" buyer, the lender is not a sucker and if the house does not appraise, well there goes the sale and the good-will you are trying to create.

My advice is to think clearly when given a listing opportunity. Make a sound business decision as to whether this is the right listing for you. And remember that you are in this business to sell listings, not plant signs in homeowner's yards. *"You have to List to Last"* as the old saying goes but that is only true if your listings sell or you capture buyers that buy. Neither will happen if you have an overpriced, under-shown, poorly conditioned house on the market.

The old saying in real estate is, *"location, location, location"*. I don't buy it. In my opinion it is always about *"price, price and price!"* For example: If I had a one quarter acre lot for sale that was located in a severely depressed area of a city but I was offering that lot for $50.00 would you buy it, probably. And if I were to offer it for $500.00 would you still buy it, probably again... How about $1,000 or $10,000? At some point the price would not be worth it. Sure the location of the home and the condition of the home are important but in my opinion it always boils down to the price of the home compared to that home's features, its location and its condition. Instead of saying, *"build it and they will come."* Maybe we should say, *"Price it right and they will come."*

I believe that if you currently have a listing and you have had no showings, there is only one reason, price. The buyers simply do not see the price of the home being worth the condition, location or features of

114

the home. No amount of advertising, marketing, open houses or Realtor lunches will overcome an improperly priced home. Since the seller can't change the location of their house, they can only change its condition or features to match the price. If that is not possible then a price reduction is inevitable if they want to sell their house. If you cannot convince the seller to adjust their price or if they agree a price reduction is necessary but they are unable to do so for economic reasons, then you must make a business decision – do you stay or do you go?

In closing, consider that in the discussion with buyers I talked about buying homes, but here I refer to selling houses, this is because in our vernacular, we sell "houses" and we buy "homes". A subtle difference I admit but if you think of the embroidered artwork found in many homes it never says, *"Welcome to our house."* Home is where we raise our family. A house is an impersonal object we are trying to rid ourselves of. When talking with buyers use the word home to create an emotional state but when working with sellers use the word house to aid the seller in disassociating themselves from the property.

What to say to sellers and how to list property

There are four important questions to ask a prospective seller at the beginning of each meeting. By asking these questions you can often zoom in on major objections a seller may have regarding the sale of their house and just as quickly find their major motivators. Consider utilizing these questions at the beginning of a listing presentation:

- *"What is the #1 reason you want sell?"*
- *"What is the #1 reason you wouldn't want to sell?"*
- *"What is your main concern about selling your property?"*
- *"What is your main concern about hiring a Realtor?"*

You need to understand what their concerns are so you can address them. You will NOT be able to move forward until you remove these objection barriers.

Let's say that their #1 concern in hiring an inexperienced Realtor. Let's see how Amy handles it...

Amy the agent: *"Mr. Seller what is your #1 concern regarding working with a Realtor?"*

Sam the seller: *"Experience, I don't want someone who is inexperienced"*

Amy the agent: *"I can certainly understand that, what is your concern with hiring an inexperienced agent?"*

Sam seller: *"I'm afraid they don't know what they are doing."*

Amy: *"That would be bad. What leads you to believe that?"*

Sam: *"Well, they don't have much experience so how do they know what forms to fill out, how to market the home, etc..."*

Amy: *"So it's important to you to make sure the agent you're working with knows what forms to complete and how to market your home."* (this is called parroting)

Sam: *"Yep. I'm not interested in holding their hand"*

Amy: *"There sure are a lot of forms, contracts and addendums to keep track of that's for sure; sounds like a checklist is important to keep all that straight. Wouldn't you agree?"*

Sam: *"Yep."*

Amy: *"I agree, that's why I use one and review all my listings with my BIC to assure we haven't missed anything. The first thing we'll need to complete is the Property Review Form. Can you give me a tour so I can fill it in?"* Amy says this as she's reaching for her form. Also note how Amy *assumed* things are fine and if he agrees to the tour we're on the right track.

After the tour our story continues...

Amy: *"Earlier you mentioned that marketing was important to you."* (This also shows she actively listened!!)

Sam: *"Yes, I <u>need</u> to sell this and I want to make sure it's getting maximum exposure."*

Amy: *"I agree, may I ask you a question? Where do you think most buyers are going to look for homes?"* (Always ask permission before asking a question)

Sam: *"The internet"*

116

Amy: *"That is very perceptive of you.* (Or words to this affect to acknowledge his insight.) *You're right. So exposing the home to as many websites as possible is important to you. It usually takes 24 – 48 hours for the MLS to send and refresh the various websites it sends to. However, I can put your house on my website tonight."*

Sam: *"Hmmm, what websites did you say it goes to?"* Amy pulls out her list of the many sites. And then restates. *"You mentioned earlier that you need to sell. I'll update the MLS tonight and you'll be able to see an initial review of your house on my website tonight but it will take a day or two for the MLS to populate to all the other websites I monitor. What is your timeframe for selling?"*

Sam: *"Within the next few months. Definitely within six months."* Notice he didn't object to you posting the listing on your website so you're most likely on the right track...

Amy: *"We need to get started then."* While pulling out her listing agreement, Amy then asks a series of questions to gently press for the listing:

- *"Please tell me again how to spell your last name"*
- *"Is there any personal property you're planning to leave, we'll want to reflect that in the listing agreement."*
- *"Are you the sole owner?"*
- *"What price were you thinking of asking?"*

What might you say at this point?

_____

_____

_____

_____

_____

_____

Amy would now proceed forward. If Sam objects, Amy stops and listens to the objections and then goes through the *"Why is that important to you?"* series of questions again.

Amy's approach is essentially circling through the following:
- Restating and repeating back the concern.
- Asking why it is important (sometimes you have to cycle a couple of times to get to their true "why").
- Restating, acknowledging, and repeating back the important issue. Acknowledging the problem exists and they have a right to their concern is critical! If they believe that YOU believe they have a right to their concern and that you want to help address it, they will be much more open to working with you. To say, "*Oh don't worry about that....*" is the verbal equivalent of a slap in the face. To deny someone their right to their concern essentially affords you one way out… the front door. You may as well pack your bags and leave.
- Addressing the concern (i.e. "*sounds like a checklist is important to you*").
- Taking an action step to address the concern (i.e. pulling the checklist out and asking to see the house).

Getting a listing is a lot like being a therapist. The therapist usually knows what the issue is long before the patient wants to recognize it or even sees it. However, the therapist simply can't say, "*You know what your problem is?*" (Although, I suppose, that question would considerably shorten their therapy sessions and regrettably, lighten their wallets because they wouldn't have any clients left.) They must act like a trail guide and steer the patient to draw their own conclusion. The same goes for you. "*You should list with me*" might work for Obi Wan Kenobi of Star Wars movie fame, but the technique doesn't work for therapists and it rarely works for Realtors.

If the seller has not clearly indicated that they are interested in listing their house with you, keep exploring with open-ended questions and utilize closing techniques to test the waters. You know you want the listing and they know you want the listing. Your entire discussion needs to center around this fact. It is the bear in the room (the common phrase of course is, "elephant in the room" but I rather doubt we would cross paths with an elephant on the AT. So, with your permission, I'd like to keep these animals in their proper place.) so embrace it, don't pretend it is not there. There is no other reason for you to be there except to get the listing; with this in mind...

Believe you already have the listing

From the moment you park in front of the seller's house, you should believe you already have the listing. Much like the therapist who already knows the problem, you will lead the conversation to bring the seller to what you already know – that you have the listing. In many ways it is the same as the trail guide who is leading you down a trail they have travelled many times; you may not know where the trail leads, but they do and they know exactly how to get you to the trail's end. This is not a form of arrogance; the trail-guide is not arrogant simply because she already knows where the trail leads even if the hiker doesn't. As with any professional, she is simply leading the way to the expected outcome.

How will the conversation go? Who knows, but by believing your sign is already in the yard and the listing is in the MLS, you will act differently, ask different questions and project a demeanor other agents won't because they believe they are in competition to get the listing you already have.

You won't need to be hyper-alert with your polished dog and pony show and your scripted responses and lines. You will simply have a conversation in a relaxed manner putting yourself and the seller at ease.

Listing prep steps

- Have multiple listing packages ready and in the trunk of your car (get a small file organizer).

- Know exactly where you're going. You should plan to drive the route the day before (preferably at the same time to assess unexpected traffic issues) so you'll be calm (or at least calmer) as you go to the listing appointment.

- Go into the MLS and put in all the information you can for the listing (including the expected list price) create the public/agent remarks and fill in the other appropriate fields; after all you have the listing don't you? (You can edit all you want, just **don't** publish the listing. You can skip this step if you don't feel comfortable. However, you are not saving nor publishing the listing, you are simply going through the motions just as an Olympic skier sees himself hurtling down the hill flying past gate after gate before he actually does hurtle down the hill (If you've never seen Olympic downhill skiing, be prepared to be awed!)).

- As much as possible, create the brochure-box flier.

- Visualize the meeting. Sit quietly and envision how you want the conversation to go. See yourself and the seller walking the path. You don't have to imagine putting the sign in the yard because it's already there. In fact, you can imagine putting an "under contract" rider on the sign. Imagine driving up and seeing the sign and brochure box in the yard. The more imaginative and visual your thoughts, the more the conversation and meeting will go exactly as you envisioned.

Years ago I had a brief stint selling mutual funds and life insurance. We used to cold call before the National Do-Not-Call Registry existed. Looking back I think I would choose door number two's "No frills, colicky baby, non-stop flight to Australia" package over cold calling. However, one memorable call did result in an appointment, so I practiced visualizing the conversation before I met with the prospect. During the meeting I began to get goose bumps because the conversation was literally going word for word just as I had envisioned it. It was a highly successful meeting and it cemented my belief that visualization works if you embrace it.

Since you both know why you're there, why not put it right out in the open. After all, would you start hiking a trail with a friend and not tell them where the trail leads? Although, I suppose it does depend on the friend.

Try this as your conversation starter:
"Mr. and Mrs. Seller, I'm here this evening to talk with you about listing your property. Is that what you want to talk about too?"

But what if they say, *"no."* That's good isn't it? After all, when would you rather find this out, two minutes into the conversation or after two hours of time spent talking with a property owner who has no intention of listing their house?

Here's a bonus, if they do say *"no"* right up front, then ask them this simple question:
"Ok, why are we meeting?" You might discover they merely want to pick your brain. That's ok, now you can help them, make a friend, make a contact, create a future opportunity, and spend 10 minutes of your time, not two hours.

Assuming they say *"yes"*, even if you're in competition, you've laid out where the trail terminates. Since you both know where you're going and have both agreed to it, you can now walk the trail together. If the conversation veers it's easy to say *"I'm sorry, I thought we were here to talk about me/my company listing your property."* or words to that affect. In other words, we got off the path for a moment so it's time to get back on.

Ok so we tamed the bear in the room. We all know why we're here and where the path is going. Now what? Remember, you know where the stumbling blocks are because you've already had the conversation in your head and you've already been down this path. In other words, there are more bears so let's go ahead and find them too. After all, when you identify one bear a smaller one may appear, but it is still blocking your path.

A quick side trail to discuss the merits of *"yes"* VS *"no"*
The old sales rule that states a *"no"* is just as good as a *"yes"* has some truth to it. Although no is not the answer we like to hear, depending on how we worded the question. It is not fair to

121

say a no is simply a veiled yes; in fact, no does means, well, no. However, there is one very positive aspect of hearing no, it means they are engaged in the conversation and as such you have an opportunity to explore your differences and find common ground or agree to disagree and walk away from the meeting. If they are non-responsive or non-committal it means they do not care. Remember that the opposite of love is not hate, it is apathy. An uncommitted, uncaring seller is, you'll forgive me, the kiss of death.

Worried about getting the listing? Write out your worries…
A recent study was conducted on students preparing for the PSAT and SAT high school exams. They asked students to write down their worries about the exam a few minutes before taking the exam. Those that wrote out their worries improved their scores a whole letter grade. Although they didn't or couldn't say why it works, I personally believe it works because it gives your mind a specific set of problems to solve. As such, it stops worrying and starts focusing on solving the problem. I believe it also gives your mind an opportunity to travel down that trail looking at the worst case scenarios so when you actually do take that walk, your fears don't play out nearly as frightfully as you imagined, so you breathe a sigh of relief, relax, and become more confident.

I think this can work extremely well for us. Before meeting with a seller, or buyer for that matter, write down your worries about the upcoming presentation.

Collecting valuable flora OR a discussion about your commission

How do we find the next bear? Ask the following:
"Mr. and Mrs. Seller, what is the biggest issue you have in hiring a real estate agent to help you sell your house?"
Whatever the answer, ask *"why?"* the why is the bear!

For example:
You: *"what is the biggest issue…?"*
Seller: *"The commission."*

You: *"Why is the commission a concern for you?"*
Seller *"I don't think you're worth it, you charge too much, the last agent didn't do anything, etc..."*

Can you see why asking *"why"* helped you identify the bear blocking your path? Now you can either tame the bear or, if that's not possible, run like heck. Oh and a good rule to remember is that you don't have to run faster than the bear, you only need to run faster than the person you're with.

What are the magic words at this point? There aren't any because every "why" from every seller is different but at least you know the issue and you can have a conversation with the seller as to why it's a concern and how they would like to resolve it. You could now ask:

- *"May I ask why you feel we're not worth it?"*
- *"What about your last agent concerned you?"*
- *"Why do you feel we charge too much?"*

And on we go peeling back the layers to find out the bear isn't quite as big as we thought.

There are many scripts and dialogs provided by many very successful real estate agents and sales gurus. I encourage you to review them, but know this, if you cannot stand in front of the mirror while looking yourself square in the eye and embrace the words provided to you then neither will the seller. Many of these commission argument scripts have been around for years and in my opinion simply ring hollow. For example:

"But the other company only charges 5%" says Mrs. Seller and so our script goes... *"Mr. and Mrs. Seller if company X is so willing to lower their commission how hard will they work to protect you during negotiations?"* or words to that affect.

Ok without pointing out the obvious, that if you don't work in your seller's best interest regardless of the commission you charge you are in clear violation of licensing law and NC RE Commission rules, just because a firm charges less than you and your firm does, does not mean they will simply walk away from their fiduciary duties and to indicate as such does a disservice to our industry as a whole, in my opinion...

Or

"Mr. and Mrs. Seller imagine if you could hire an attorney or a doctor who would work for you at no charge and you wouldn't have to pay them anything until you got the outcome exactly like you wanted it."

Now we're comparing our 75 hours of pre-licensing and 90 hours of post-licensing to the years of schooling doctors and lawyers endure; not to mention the thousands of dollars in student loans they incur?

Look, if you don't want to reduce your commission then simply tell them. Here has been my stock answer for years, *"Mr. and Mrs. Seller, my commission is not negotiable but thanks for asking."* Have I lost a listing because of that? Sure but I've also gotten my fair share with the seller simply saying, *"Well I had to ask..."*

Finally, I suppose if they continue to press for a commission reduction, you could point out that you are a commissioned-based salesperson who, in the past, was paid nothing when the buyer you had spent weeks with ended up buying directly from a For Sale by Owner. Or that you lost a listing even though you repeatedly pleaded with the seller to repaint the Pepto-Bismol® pink room a neutral color, only to have the seller refuse to do so but then relist with another real estate company, reduce their list price, and repaint the pink room a neutral color, where upon, miracles of miracles, the house sold in just a few short days. Or you could mention the hours you spent carefully putting together a CMA for a prospective seller, causing you to miss your son's soccer match only to have the seller change their mind and decide to list with their best friend and then have the audacity to say, *"Oh by the way thank you for performing that CMA, may we keep it?"* In fact you may decide to say to Mr. and Mrs. Seller, *"The actual listing of your home is free... I charge what I charge for all these other reasons."* You could say that but I rather doubt you should. Keep it simple, be confident, and sincere regarding what you charge and why.

A few final thoughts regarding commissions

This may sound like heresy, but in my opinion it is ok to reduce your commission; especially as a new agent. Your objective is to get listings to help you grow your business (the saying "list to last" still rings true today). Many start-up businesses reduce their prices to establish a foothold. Why should real estate agents be any different? For that matter, think about the last time you purchased something from a personal friend or family member; did they give you a discount or throw a little something in that they wouldn't normally offer?

Of course the argument you'll hear is that if you start out with reduced commissions you'll never get out of that mode because every subsequent seller will want the same commission the previous seller received. You'll be stuck at that lower commission your entire career. *"Is that what you want?!?!"* they'll warn you! Of course this argument only makes sense if each subsequent seller knew the previous one.

And even if they're right, even if you're getting listing after listing because the previous seller referred you to the next seller and so on and so forth, but you continue to grow your business on a referral-only basis at a reduced commission rate, would that really be so bad? Oh, and we haven't even mentioned all the buyer clients you've picked up who chose not to buy your listing but will utilize your services to buy another home listed by a competitor who is paying a very nice commission to buyer's agents. Should all of this happen, I apologize, please let me know and I'll send you a sympathy card. Let's face it, the odds are most of your listings will be isolated from each other so charge what you want.

⚠ **Warning:** Before agreeing to reduce your commission you must be sure you understand your firm's policy regarding commissions. Some firms will take their split based on a certain percentage.

If you agree to less than that, they will still take their split based on that pre-set commission rate, which could end up costing you a significant amount of money.

Should you find yourself in the envious position of acting as a dual agent in which you represent both the buyer and the seller in the same transaction, your commission split with your firm will be based upon the full commission amount and possibly even a bonus for selling your own listing. Should you reduce your commission? Assuming you understand your firm's policies and the buyer and/or seller is pushing you to do so, I think you should. It simply boils down to picking and choosing your battles. After all, you are representing both parties. Your firm will receive the full commission amount, of which you will take your share, and you have two clients who can provide future referral business; not to mention the future business they may personally bring when they are ready to buy and sell again. Once more though, be sure you understand your firm's policies regarding commissions before agreeing to reduce the commission amount.

I'm guessing a few of you reading this section are not terribly receptive to my thoughts about being so quick to reduce commission. I want you to know that I'm not quick to reduce my commission, and as I mentioned, I have traditionally held firm on the amount of commission I charge. However, I have also come to realize that the world of real estate has changed and I no longer consider it such a vital part of my business that I risk losing a listing over it. For me, I would rather receive a smaller percentage of something in lieu of a colossal percent of nothing. I also believe that given today's market and economic struggles, sellers are not always in a position to pay top dollar, and if by reducing the commission charged I help them lower their price for a faster sale, I'm ok with that.

But I understand, you don't want to reduce your commission and you want some scripts to use. I'm sure there are hundreds of them but here are a few:

Script 1
The buyer or seller states: *"We want you to reduce your commission."*

Reply: *"Should I assist you in getting you what you want for your home, would you be willing to pay this fee that I split with cooperating brokerage firms who may have assisted in the sale?"* (If they say *"yes"*, reply *"that's all I'm asking you to do now."*)

This script has been around for a very long time and it is essentially asking the seller if they walk away with the money they want, would they have a problem paying you your requested commission? A fair question to ask, but I can't help to think that it comes across as a bit of a head scratcher and sounds eerily like the old joke, *"So have you stopped beating your wife yet?"* (Try answering *"yes"* or *"no"* to that question!) I guess the old saying; *"If you can't dazzle them with brilliance, baffle them with bull s_ _t."* is alive and well in this script.

Script 2
If it is a money issue, *"Given the condition of the market it is important that we incent buyer agents to show your house. This fee is split with those agents. Reducing it may cause them to not be as motivated to show your home. The more buyers that see your home the greater the likelihood an offer will be made. It's a numbers game wouldn't you agree?"*

Script 3
"I understand the commission fee is a concern for you. Of course this fee amount is not payable until you actually sell your home under your terms and conditions and you receive the sales price you desire. Unlike other professions, you are not required to pay a professional fee until you are completely satisfied with the price you receive for your home. That seems fair doesn't it?"

Script 4

"It wouldn't be a problem if you don't pay this fee until you get what you want for your home would it?" (Often times when talking with sales people, our natural inclination is to say, *"no"* this script takes advantage of that.)

As you reviewed these scripts, did they make you feel a little dirty? Like maybe you could use a long hot shower or at least a good hand scrubbing? If so, here's room to create your own scripts:

_____

_____

_____

_____

_____

_____

_____

_____

_____

_____

_____

_____

_____

_____

_____

_____

_____

_____

_____

_____

_____

_____

_____

_____

_____

On to the next bear:
"Are there any other issues that would prevent you from hiring me?" if there are, ask *"why"* and rinse and repeat until you've discovered smaller and smaller bears or until you've gotten to the tiniest of those Russian nesting dolls (my apologies for the mixed metaphor).

Once you've tamed the last bear, you may want to ask, *"Based on where we are, is it fair to say you're ready to move forward?"* if they say *"yes"*, start filling in the listing paperwork. If they say *"no"*, another bear popped up and needs to be addressed.

In conclusion, practice, practice, and practice; when you find the specific words to say, that you feel comfortable with and address the consumers concern, practice them so they become a part of you.

You successfully tamed all the bears OR what do you do now that you have the listing

You procured your first listing, congratulations! Now what? Your firm should provide a listing checklist to ensure all of the necessary tasks associated with that listing are completed in a timely manner and done in the proper order. This book is not intended to replace that list so be sure to check with your BIC for a copy of their listing checklist. However, regardless of the firm you join, there are a few items I recommend you do with each and every listing.

Week one
- Put the expiration date in your calendar. Agents do forget the expiration date and I have called expired listings only to have the seller explode (figuratively, of course, not literally) when I told them their listing had expired and their agent hadn't even notified them. And I must admit that I too did that one time. The seller was very forgiving, but I was very embarrassed! By the way, isn't it interesting that the word embarrass ends with the pronunciation "bare ass" which is often how we see ourselves in those situations. Moving on…

- Be sure your seller receives a copy of all listing information and contracts.

- Immediately send the seller a hand-written thank you note and include your business card.

- Follow up with an emailed copy of the MLS listing and ask them to proof the information and share with you any concerns or suggestions they may have.

- Create and mail postcards to the homes surrounding your listing. Provide information about the listing, a picture (or two), the MLS number, and the list price. In my opinion, the days of hiding listing information from the buyers, with the hope they will call you, are over. Requiring a potential buyer to call so they can find out the list price and other essential information may result in an opportunity to talk with a prospect but will more than likely result in the buyer simply skipping the house or logging on to Zillow or Trulia.com and entering the home's address – there they will find all the information they need and by not providing that information up front, you've simply alienated the buyer. With all this said though, if it is the policy of your firm to advertise a code instead of the MLS number and list price then obey that firm's policy or find a new firm.

- Take photographs on a day when the lighting is ideal. But in any case, take at least one photograph of the front of the house as soon as you can. I have seen more than my fare share of listings in the MLS with no photograph; yet they have been on the market for weeks if not months. Buyers (as do Realtors) simply skip these listings and keep looking. Unless the seller does not want a photograph in the MLS, there is no excuse not to have at least one of them in the MLS at the time you list the property.

130

- Put your flyers together and provide copies to the seller. Include the MLS number and price (see my thoughts above). I like to make the brochures a seller responsibility since they are the first to know if the box is empty. If, however, the seller is unable or unwilling, place a notice on your calendar to check the brochures once per week. Remember that the brochure box will empty out quickly in the beginning of the listing period as curious neighbors pilfer (I mean pick up) a few of the brochures.

Subsequent weeks

- Perform a new CMA four to six weeks out; particularly if you have had no showings and share the results with the seller.

- Regularly update your MLS pictures. For example, if it is now July 2nd and you still display exterior photos taken back in February when there was snow on the ground and no leaves on the trees, how closely will the seller think you're monitoring their listing?

- Keep a log of the agents who have shown the house and chronicle their comments. Create an email group contact list and update these agents should you have a price change. It is very possible that their buyers have not yet made a buying decision and the price change may very well be the catalyst that pushes them to make an offer. Do not expect that agent to keep up with your listing just because they showed it in the past. Take the initiative to be sure they have the latest information about your listing.

- If you have had a listing for several months, re-read your remarks and agent remarks in the MLS and update as needed. For example, if you're still advertising *"Great listing, won't last long..."* you may want to consider removing that comment if you have been on the market for 250 days. Recently I saw a listing on the market for over 400 days and the words *"... won't last long..."* were still in the agent's remarks field. Is it reasonable to believe that this listing agent is actively monitoring this listing? I don't think so.

- Contact the seller after the first showing and ask if the showing instructions they provided are working OK. If not, correct and update the showing service provider.

- I am not a huge proponent of babysitting the seller. I am not one to call every day just to check in. However, you do need to check in occasionally and consistently. Discuss with the seller what that process will be. Be cautious about asking them how often they would like to be contacted or you may be calling them every day. If you are at a listing appointment, consider saying something like, *"Mr. and Mrs. Seller, as part of my service, I provide weekly updates either by email or phone call. Please know that there may be weeks when there is little to report but I will still provide you with that update each Thursday. I will add that responsibility to my calendar this evening."* This statement is known as an assumptive close which we'll talk more about later. You can see that I did not ask permission or request their input and should they allow me to continue, I'm on the right track to get the listing.

Vacant listings

If your seller has already moved and the home is vacant, be sure to plan for the following:

- Is the grass and landscaping being maintained?

- Are the mail and/or newspaper picked up regularly?

- Visit the home at least once per week. Walk the exterior and interior. Check for:
    - Un-flushed or dare I say, under-flushed toilets.
    - Burnt out light bulbs. Carry low-wattage spare bulbs in your car.

- Cobwebs /dust. Yes you should perform some light dusting, in case you were wondering.
- Pick up business cards from previous showings and add to your contact list.
- Gently spray with room freshener if there is a musty smell.
- Check all windows and doors to be sure they are locked.
- Check the thermostat to be sure it hasn't been turned off or the settings have been changed. There is nothing worse than burst pipes while the home was under your watch.
- Discuss your visit with the seller during your regular check-in meeting.
- Peek under the crawl space for burst pipes, fallen insulation, scraps of wood or even stray cats (I actually encountered a mummified cat while crawling under a home and no I won't share with you my reaction or the word I uttered or why I was under there.)

- Who will be responsible for the flyers? Consider having the owner ask a neighbor to restock the flyers.

Your listing received an offer

Great joy and trepidation accompanies your first offer and your one hundredth offer for that matter. Keep in mind that it is, after all, only an offer. You have a long way to go before closing and your commission check clears. Once again, this book is not designed to replace the advice of your BIC or your future firm's office policies regarding the handling of offers but I have a few suggestions and thoughts to keep in mind.

I have found that the first offer is usually one of the better offers and one of the more interested buyers. They may have had their eye on the home and/or they may have visited the home, fell in love and quickly wrote an offer. Even if this occurs, this offer and any subsequent offers can come in many shapes and sizes:

Low ball offers: Even strongly interested buyers may present a low ball offer. Encourage the seller to counter-offer back – even if that counter-offer is at full list price. Rejecting any offer simply closes the door on what could ultimately be a successful sale. I have had my share of low ball offers in which the buyer was merely fishing. Countering back at full price showed the buyer the seller was not desperate and on more than one occasion the buyer came around and presented a serious second offer. Always encourage your seller to make a counter-offer even if the buyer's offer was, on the surface, insulting.

Cash offers: They say, *"cash is king"*, but often a buyer who is getting a loan is better than a cash buyer, because the buyer obtaining a loan has paid a loan application fee and therefore has some skin in the game. If the buyer is presenting cash, be sure to ask for proof of funds.

Offers the seller is willing to accept at first glance. This certainly can make life easy but ask yourself, if you presented an offer that was accepted with no questions asked, how would you feel? A buyer may experience buyer's remorse should the seller accept their offer with no questions asked. Should you counter-offer? Possibly, it depends on the offer, the buyer, and the seller – just recognize that offers accepted at first blush may end up with a buyer asking for the moon once inspections start and/or one of the party's suffering from regret.

Full price offers: *"Obviously"*, thinks the seller, *"We were under-priced."* Maybe or maybe not, if you've done your homework the more likely answer is the home was priced correctly. Should you receive a full price offer, be sure to bring comparables with you to review with the seller.

Multiple offers: Always get your seller's permission to reveal to the buyers that they are in a multiple offer environment. You do not have the unilateral right to disclose this information without first obtaining your seller's permission. Discuss with the seller what their options are: reject all offers, counter-offer to all offers, counter-offer to some, and reject others, and of course you should warn them not to accept more than one offer or they will have sold their home multiple times – a very sticky

134

situation indeed. Has this ever happened? Yes. Was it ugly? I'm sure it was, let's not find out the hard way.

Shopping offers: You may never reveal to one buyer what another buyer has offered without the previous buyer's permission and what buyer, in their right mind, would give permission to reveal their offer's content. Be extremely cautious what you say to other agents in the transaction, particularly if you have a buyer who is also making an offer (i.e. you are acting as a dual agent). Document all of your conversations with all parties.

Congratulations, the seller is under contract
- Once you are under contract, be sure to put the closing date and the Due Diligence Period expiration dates in your calendar.

- Be sure you are in regular communication with the other agent. Even if they don't call you, contact them and ask if there is anything you can do to help or are there any questions you can answer. Remember, they have other clients and your phone call may prompt them to remember to set up the inspections they forgot to schedule.

- Place an Under Contract rider on your sign.

- Send out Under Contract postcards to the same homes you sent the Just Listed postcards to. I know it is old-fashioned but it still works; particularly since people have fewer and fewer pieces of mail to sort through.

- Update your Comparable Market Analysis. Remember we are not allowed to hire appraisers but we are allowed to talk with them and provide justification for the contracted sales price.

- Be sure the seller is aware of any inspection dates as they come up.

- Update the listing status on the MLS and check all the various websites to be sure they have been updated as well. Note that not all of them will auto-refresh in a way, if any way, that ensures an accurate portrayal of your listing. You are ultimately responsible for that true and accurate picture.

- Discuss with the seller and the buyer's agent when the buyer will receive the house keys. Should you slide the keys across the closing table into the buyer's waiting hands or hold on to the keys until the deed has been recorded? I mention this predicament here because the best time to discuss the transference of keys is when you go under contract, not when you are sitting at the closing table. Imagine the buyer at the closing table physically, emotionally, and mentally exhausted ready to take possession of their new home only to find out that they will not get the keys until the deed has been recorded and since it is 4 PM the deed will not be recorded until tomorrow (assuming, of course, tomorrow isn't Saturday).

There is no rule or law that says the buyer cannot receive the keys to their new home prior to the deed being recorded but it is both good and safe practice to avoid giving the buyer the keys until the deed has been recorded.

⚐ Discuss the transference of keys with the seller, the buyer and/or the buyer's agent when you go under contract so that all parties can plan accordingly.

Trail log:

_____

_____

_____

_____

_____

_____

_____

_____

Chapter 12: Finding the best views OR working with buyers and showing properties.

Many of the techniques we've used with sellers can also be applied to buyers.

I believe the number one mistake agents make when showing properties is to make statements that are blatantly obvious, as in *"So Mr. and Mrs. Buyer, this is the kitchen, and here's the living room. Oh and look, here is the back patio."* My goodness, unless your client is visually impaired you're really not bringing much to the table. In fact since they have already previewed the home online they most likely know where the kitchen, living room and patio are before you even enter the home.

So what do we say? This is where actively listening and understanding your buyer's true wants and desires becomes so critical. Hopefully you've already had your exploratory conversation with questions like:

- *"How do you use your home, kitchen and other rooms now?"*
- *"Why are you looking to purchase a home?"*
- *"What are the 3 most important features of a home to you and why?"* (The why discovers the benefits to the buyer.)

Your questions:

_____

_____

_____

_____

 Remember buyers don't purchase homes for the features, they purchase homes for the benefits those features provide. For example: The big back yard is the feature; a place for their children to run around and get their nervous energy out so they can sleep at night is the benefit.

137

That's why it is so important to ask "why" based questions. If all you know is that they want a big backyard and there aren't any homes with that feature available are you out of luck? Not if you know the why! The condominium building down the street with tight security and a full gym, pool, and play area might also enable that nervous energy to be released. Or the small yarded home within walking distance to the community pool/basketball court may work fine.

In my opinion, very little of your conversation, when you go through a home should be about the features. The conversation should be more about how that home's features can benefit the buyer. If you are unsure what the buyer's benefit needs are, don't ask *"isn't this a lovely X"* instead ask *"how do you see yourself using this kitchen, living room, etc... and why is that important to you?"*

It is true that when a buyer starts mentally placing furniture in a room that it is a good sign they are interested in the home, but don't ask, *"Where do you see the TV in this room?"* instead ask, *"Where do you see yourself sitting for optimal viewing of your next Panther's game party you have each weekend?"* Or *"If we have the seller remove that interior wall to open the area between the kitchen and den wouldn't this home provide more room and better viewing for your next Panthers party?"*
(You see, in your exploratory meeting you discovered they are huge fans and they like to throw Panther game day parties.)

 Showing homes is all about features and benefits. What's the feature and how does it benefit the buyer. You cannot know this without spending time with the buyer and asking open-ended questions.

They can see the features but they can't always catch site of the benefits those features bring, so listen well and you'll help them discover benefits they hadn't even thought of.

Feature/Benefit exercise
Create three benefits for a prospective buyer for each of the following features:

Feature	Benefits
Small bathroom	1.
	2.
	3.
Master Bedroom downstairs	1.
	2.
	3.
Master Bedroom upstairs	1.
	2.
	3.
Screened in porch but no deck for gas grill	1.
	2.
	3.
(Here's a tricky one) the home is perfect but next to a busy road	1.
	2.
	3.

Large kitchen but dated   1.

                                          2.

                                          3.

The ugly duckling

Ok, so the buyer hates the home the moment you pull up to it. In fact they don't even let you slow down… Slow down anyway. Stop the car and if it is protocol in your market, notify the buyer that you need to drop off a business card so the seller knows you kept your showing appointment. Invite the buyer to come in with you. You never know, the front of the home may not be all that appealing but they may fall in love with the interior or the Jacuzzi on the back deck that the listing agent failed to mention. Further, you may discover new features and the benefits they bring to the buyer. They may hate the home but love a feature that can now be included in future searches.

Learning about the local fauna before stepping on the trail OR important questions you should always ask before showing homes

Before you put one foot in your car and they put one foot in theirs, spend time with your buyer. Get to know them. What do they like to do in their off time? Do they work out of the home and if so what do they do and what are their needs. (Warning: be sure the HOA CC&R's allow for the type of home based business activity your buyer needs to conduct.) Buying a home, only then to find out the business they are operating is not allowed does not a good deal make!

Even something as innocuous as a CPA could be a problem. Where I used to live a CPA worked out of his home and was ordered to cease and desist because of the number of cars parked on the street during the CPA's busy season. He ended up moving his business to rented office space. That could have been devastating had he not already built a large client base with the resultant income stream.

Does your client like to cook or entertain? They may say they want a small kitchen because they don't cook but they do love to entertain. Most parties end up congregating to the kitchen so even though they don't cook they may still need a large kitchen.

Spend more time with your client in your office, in a coffee house or at their current residence getting to know their true housing wants and needs and you'll spend less time in the car. Begin your housing search with the following types of questions:

- *What is your main concern about purchasing a property, financing, etc..."*
  (Why ask this question? Because if you don't understand their main concerns you may never figure out why they didn't like house number 1, 2, 3, and 4. It wasn't that they didn't like them, they were simply scared of the home buying process but you never discovered that because you didn't ask... Oops.)

- *"What's the #1 reason you would buy this home?"*
  (You're not necessarily asking them to buy this home but you are looking for positive feedback on the features and benefits to the buyer to help you narrow your future searches.)

- *"What's the #1 reason you wouldn't buy this home?"*
  (You guessed it; you're looking for the negative feedback to eliminate those features from your next MLS search.)

- *"If this home fell off the market tomorrow morning because someone wrote an offer that was accepted today, how would you feel?"*
  (This question has worked really well for me in the past! We ask how they "feel" because buying a home is an emotional decision. If the reply is they would be upset, hurt, angry, or sad, skip everything and suggest they write up the offer. If their response is *"We'd be ok.*

141

No problem. " You probably need to keep looking.)

- *"How do you see yourself using this kitchen, deck, family room, basement etc...? "*
  (It is more important to know how a buyer will use a home rather than knowing they want a 3 BR, 2 BA house. Because if we understand their BIG WHY's we'll have a better and quicker understanding of the home that suits their needs, faster and more efficient searches, less time in the car, and quicker closings. Sounds pretty good don't you think?)

Which trail has the best view OR keeping track of the homes you show

One of the biggest frustrations when showing homes is keeping track of which home had which feature. If you show too many homes, the buyer will end up literally creating a home that contains the best of all the features they saw that day. Now I'm sure the home they've created is quite lovely but unless they are prepared to build it, it probably doesn't exist. I recommend that you show no more than four homes per day. By doing so, it will be easier to clearly remember the features each home has to offer. Further, by limiting the number of showings to just four homes, you will be better able to provide productive feedback to the listing agent because you'll have a better memory of the home.

However, regardless of the number homes you show, create a showing page that contains the following information and keep a copy in your buyer's folder:

- Address, price, MLS# fields
- #BR, BA, other vital statistics fields
- How they plan to use the home (write in section)
- Note section for writing buyer comments
- 2 LARGE check boxes
  - *Is this home on your list?*
  - *Is this home off your list?*

142

- Put the pages in an inexpensive clipboard and give it to the buyer to fill out. At the end of the day, make copies and give them to the buyer or scan them in and email their copies.
- Assuming the property is on the list ask them, *"What is the maximum you would pay for this home?"* Why ask this question? Because it helps you understand how serious they are and where the home really is on their list. It's a relatively non-threatening question because you're not asking them to make an offer, just what they would be willing to pay.
- If they are willing to pay close to asking price, this is when you should press to write up the offer.

How do I get to the spectacular view from here OR asking for the order

Many agents have outstanding listing and buyer presentations; they explain the Working with Real Estate Agents Brochure as if they had written it themselves. They truly understand their buyer's wants and needs but they never get around to asking for that buyer's business. I would like to put to rest a myth that I believe persists in our industry... *"Asking for the order is rude and pushy and just may alienate the client. I wouldn't want it done to me so why would I do it to my client? When they are ready they will tell me."* The next time you are at a restaurant see how long it takes you to order your meal if the waiter takes this approach and fails to ask you if you are ready to order.

Asking people for business is not rude; it is simply a logical conclusion to a conversation regarding the purchase and sale of virtually anything, including real estate. The way you ask may be rude and you may need to work on that but the fact that you ask is simply part of the process. Please ask for the order.

Sometimes buyers make your life easy and they tell you they're ready to write an offer. If this happens, STOP talking and START writing.

Several years ago I needed a new roof so I asked a roofing company to stop by and give me a quote. I was very impressed with the

143

representative, the price, and the quality of the product. On two separate occasions I made it clear I was ready to go forward with the order yet the representative continued with his presentation. I finally had to give a time-out signal, look the representative in the eye, and say, *"Stop talking, you have my business, where do I sign?"* I can assure you not every buyer will be that obvious and some may simply find another agent who is willing to pick up on their subtle clues and give them the occasional push they need to make a buying decision.

Trail log:

_____

_____

_____

_____

_____

_____

_____

_____

_____

_____

_____

_____

_____

_____

_____

_____

_____

_____

_____

_____

_____

_____

_____

_____

_____

Chapter 13: Convincing others to carry your backpack OR closing techniques.

As a Realtor you have fiduciary duties to your clients and you are to conduct yourself according to the Realtor Code of Ethics – both of which puts your client's needs above your own. This does not mean, however, that you must avoid giving your clients an occasional nudge to make smart decisions. Just as the mother bird has to shove her young from the nest for their first flight, you may need to "shove" your clients to take their first, second, or even third flight into the housing market. Essentially what I am talking about is closing techniques.

There are many types of closing techniques and a variety of resources to learn about them but I would like to discuss those that I have found to be very effective. Please understand that by saying, *"What's it gonna take to get you in this house today?"* may be a classic hard sale closing technique but it is certainly not one that I advocate.

I believe that agents sometimes shy away from closing techniques because they feel they are being pushy and that the buyer or seller will make their decision in due course. And this may be true but they may not make their decision with **you** if you don't occasionally check in with them.

Essentially that is what closing techniques allow you to do… check in with your client to see how they are doing and where they are in their buying and selling decision making process. If you wait until the end of a listing appointment to close you have, in effect, gone down an unfamiliar trail with no map and no way of knowing where you really are. You're only hope is that you guessed right and the trail led you to where you wanted to go. Closing techniques are nothing more than trail blaze markers along the way that ensure you're on the right trail and you're heading in the right direction. If you feel uncomfortable using closing techniques, you're not using the right ones.

The alternative close

Funny, we do this one with our children all the time. Do you want this box of cereal or that box of cereal? By narrowing the choices to only two, it clears away the clutter and makes it easier for the child to make a decision. Adults are really nothing more than big kids so clear away the clutter and give them a narrow choice. (For example, *"Would tomorrow morning or afternoon work better for you to discuss listing your property?"* or *"The builder is offering granite or Corian® counter tops, which would you prefer?"*)

The "I'll get back to you" close

Often in listing appointments the seller wants time to think about what you have discussed and to decide whether they want to list their property with you and your firm. This is certainly understandable because in their mind it is a decision that goes well beyond putting the sign in the yard. Their decision involves realizing a major chapter in their life is about to close and a new one is about to start; that the years of memories piled throughout the house will need to be purged, packed away, forgotten or left behind. For many this has been the home in which they have raised their children, lost a loved one, laughed, cried, and fought. To them, this isn't a listing, this is their life.

Over time, we as agents become numbed or jaded or we simply stop focusing on what is truly going through the sellers' minds when we list their homes. Heck, we do it all the time, what's the big deal. To many sellers it's the "biggest deal" they've ever faced. Please remember this the next time you meet with a seller to list their house.

I learned the hard way that if you don't establish rapport with a seller, you cannot begin to advise them on changes they need to make to prepare their home for sale. I had been on a roll listing several properties in only a few short days. I was feeling cocky and on top of my game. At one particular appointment I met with Mr. and Mrs. Seller to discuss listing their home. I was in competition with two other firms and another agent from my own office but I felt confident that I would get the listing. While we sat at the kitchen table, the question came up as to what they

146

might do to prepare their home for sale. Without hesitation I started rattling off ideas as if we were three co-workers discussing ways to improve our product line.

What happened next taught me a significant life lesson. As I was pontificating, Mrs. Seller began to cry. Mr. Seller gave me a look that could only be read as, *"What the hell have you done to my wife?"* I did not get the listing and, to rub salt in the wound I had created, the sellers listed with my firm but with the other agent who sat two desks down from me. To be sure the wound was sufficiently painful, the home sold four days later. Ouch!

What had I done wrong? I did not establish the rapport necessary to put us all on the same team. I was still the agent and they were still the sellers. I was still the one wanting the commission and they were the ones still holding on to the dreams they had created. I was selling a "house" and they were selling their "home". To you the listing appointment may only be a couple of hours of your time and a pile of paperwork. To the sellers it is a lifetime of memories. Never forget this.

But I digress. Let's get back to the "I'll get back to you" closing technique. This technique, sometimes called the adjournment close, gives the seller breathing room while creating enough tension for them to want to make a decision. Hollywood has made a living with the adjournment close – especially during the old serial westerns our parents and grandparents watched in movie theaters; the movie always ended with the hero hanging from a cliff (thus the term cliff hanger) or in some other peril with the voice-over guy saying, *"What will our hero do?"* the movie faded to black, the theater lights came on, and the movie goers were left breathless and desperately waiting for the next show – this is the essence of an adjournment close.

Of course your first girlfriend or boyfriend did it naturally. The excitement builds and you're ready for your first kiss when they pull away and tell you they'll call you tomorrow. They have just conducted an adjournment close and a tap dance on your heart.

If you believe you have a good shot at creating a client relationship but you also believe that pressing them to sign papers is not going to be productive or could result in potential ill-will between you and your hoped for client, strike first… Simply state, *"I see that you are thinking about this very important decision. Why don't I call you tomorrow and we will set up a follow up meeting."* At this point begin to pack your items. One of two things is going to happen. They will either agree with your idea or they will ask you to hold on, they will confer, and then say something like, *"No, we're good we don't need more time. Let's write up the paperwork."* Unpack and complete your paperwork.

You are effectively creating a pressurized environment full of potential excitement but then releasing some of that pressure on behalf of the buyer or seller. Interestingly they appreciate that and will repay you by giving you the opportunity to come back.

Can this technique back-fire? Sure. You have to have reasonable confidence that they will hire you to sell their home or that the buyer will write an offer but you also sense they need more time.

The "We hate losing" close
This closing technique phrases statements and questions to address our fear of immediate loss VS our desire for future gain. When I sold life insurance and mutual funds, this technique was used to ask the "mark" (uh, I mean potential policy holder*), "If you were going to start saving money, when would you start?"* I have since used a variation of this question to assist a buyer in starting their loan application by asking, *"Mr. and Mrs. Buyer, interests rates are at historic lows, you may be losing money by not applying for a loan now. Wouldn't you agree?"* Or if I think they are ready to make an offer I may say, *"Mr. and Mrs. Buyer, home prices are very low right now. You'll most likely lose money if you wait, because prices will eventually rise."*

One reason the above statements can be effective, is because, in general, people fear immediate loss over the possibility of future gain. In other words, by saying, *"You are losing money by not buying a home today."* you will generate a higher likelihood of action by the buyer rather than pronouncing, *"You can save money by buying a home today."* Even though they are, in essence, the same statements, the first talks about what is happening today (*"...you are losing money"*) whereas the second statement talks about what could happen in the future (*"...you can save money"*). By and large when you point out the loss they are experiencing today as opposed to the gain they could see tomorrow, the consumer's tendency will be to act to avoid the loss, rather than act to experience a future gain.

Economists call this phenomenon loss aversion. Because we can't predict what will happen tomorrow, our preference is to not lose what we have today. It is one reason investors have a tendency to sell low and buy high (The opposite, of course, of what they should do. Although, it should be noted that this investment strategy tends to be short-lived; not because the investor learns, but because after it has been employed a few times, there is no money left with which to invest.) It is also the reason, I presume, children will agree to one cookie today rather than waiting for two cookies tomorrow.

In general, we simply cannot wait for a future event that may, or may not, result in a gain; so instead we take what we can get today. The phrase, "cut your losses" seems to encapsulate this concept perfectly. But even when our losses ARE losses, we tend to favor them over the potential of a future gain.

Instead of phrasing your questions that ask the buyer or seller to take into consideration the possibility of a future gain, ask questions that reveal their fear of an immediate loss. Certainly you should not act underhandedly by taking advantage of society's propensity toward loss aversion, but if you know that now is the time to buy or sell yet your client is unnecessarily hesitant, rephrase your question to address the affect of an immediate loss rather than the possibility of a future gain.

The classic "Ben Franklin" close
Draw a large T on a piece of paper and put the pros on one side and the cons on the other. Don't weigh the importance of each item, simply list

them. If you are working with engineering or accounting type clients this can help them visually see why they should make their decision.

The compliment close

I must admit, I'm not terribly good at this one, I feel like people can see right through me, but my mother is a wizard with this closing technique. I cannot tell you how many times I've found myself performing a chore for her and not even knowing how I got sucked into doing it. I think mothers in general are masters at this technique. The compliment close uses flattery as a way to convince the buyer/seller that they have made the right choice and they should act. As in: *"You have excellent taste, I didn't see how the orange shag carpet highlights the avocado green refrigerator until you pointed that out. Have you ever thought about becoming an interior designer?"*

OK, that was a bit over the top. However, it can be very effective if you believe they have a valid point. If you're just making stuff up to flatter them, they'll see right through you. With this technique, you're not closing, you're simply flattering them on their intelligence, insight, taste, etc... The more flattered they feel, the more they crave to be flattered, and the more confident they become that they can and should make the decision to buy or sell.

If you want to test this technique at home and you have a child struggling with homework, while displaying a sense of awe, compliment them on something they accomplished earlier in the day and watch how their confidence builds to tackle the problem they are facing.

Be genuine with this technique. Should you bear false witness with your flattery, the old saying *"Flattery will get you everywhere"* will become *"flattery gets you nowhere!"*

Here are some samples and space for you to write a few of your own:
- *"That is a terrific idea, I look forward to..."*
- *"I would have never thought of that, what wonderful insight you have in..."*

- *"That is very perceptive of you to think of..."*
- *"With your knowledge of this business, I'm looking forward to..."*
- *"I'm really impressed on how quickly you picked up on _____ that is very perceptive of you..."*

Your "compliment close" statements:

_____
_____
_____
_____
_____
_____

Overcoming objection close

I suppose this closing technique could also be called the if/then technique. It's a bit like quid pro quo (you do this, I'll do that). This can be a very effective technique with buyers should you see they are close but there are a few nagging issues. Say something like this, *"If the seller fixes that _____, then are you ready to move forward..."* This technique is easy to remember because you need only remember two words (if/then). For example:

- *"If the seller will address the water issue in the crawl space, then do you feel this house will work for you?"*
- *"If I reduce my commission to sell your home provided you agree to work with me to buy your next home, then are you ready to complete the listing agreement paperwork?"*

Write out your if/then statements:

_____
_____
_____
_____
_____

Choice close

An effective closing technique when the seller (such as a builder) is offering options.

- *"I believe the seller is offering this counter in grey, black, or pink granite. Which do you prefer?"*
- *"The exterior trim at the front door can either be vinyl, stone, or brick. Do you have a preference?"*

I have two thoughts on this closing technique:

1. For some reason listing things in threes works best. Interior decorators encourage odd numbers of items to be grouped together instead of even numbers. As humans we seem to be oddly attracted to odd numbers and more particularly groups of three.

2. The classic shell game, in which a con artist places a pea under one of three shells and then rearranges those shells so you have to guess where the pea is, often starts with the pea being placed under the middle shell. Just as we are attracted to three, we are also attracted to the middle of the list of three. Therefore, put the most appealing item in the middle; for example, *"Would you prefer vinyl, stone, or brick?"*. (In case you're curious why we ultimately, and always, end up losing the shell game, it is because as we get more confident in our predictions, we become more willing to bet larger amounts of money; at the right time, the protagonist begins to palm the object, and apparently a substantial amount of our cash, and so the pea does not reside under any of the shells.)

The because close

A few years ago participants of a study were instructed to see if they could cut in line to make copies at a certain company's copier. Interestingly they found that if the participant simply asked to cut in line, their request was regularly denied but if the participant added a statement beginning with the word because, as in *"Because I am late for a meeting"*, the request was regularly granted. Now here is the interesting thing, even if the participant simply said, *"Because I need to make a copy."* The request was regularly granted. In other words by using the word because the participant created a reason to cut in line; even if that reason was to simply make a copy, which I presume was everyone's reason for standing in line.

If you need to reschedule a meeting or you are trying to nudge your buyer into making an offer, add a statement that begins with the word because. As in, *"Because another buyer may have seen this house yesterday, you should move forward today."*

The assumptive close

If you sense this home is "the one", there are a couple of ways you can close the deal. I think one of the most powerful yet non-intrusive approaches is called the assumptive close technique. This approach simply makes statements and/or asks questions with the assumption that they like the home and they are planning to write the offer but they just haven't told you yet. It is non-intrusive because if they respond negatively or go off like the "Grenade" you can always say, *"I'm sorry, I assumed or I thought or I inferred...".*

To use the assumptive close technique, simply ask or make statements such as the following...

- *"The inspector I use is very thorough and we can probably have him out here within a couple of days."* This is said during the showing should an issue arise or you sense they have interest. If you don't get an objection, they are interested in moving forward (move to writing the offer).

- *"To make sure I spell it correctly on the offer, how do you spell your last name?"* This assumes, of course, they don't have a name like "Smith".

153

- *"Based on what you've told me about your needs, I think this (fill in the blank) should serve your needs well. How do you feel about that?"*

- *"The movers should have no problem negotiating (fill in the blank) while they're unloading your (fill in the blank)."* This is a simple statement; the only thing you're looking for is a positive acknowledgement. If they nod their head, they probably have an interest in the home.

- *"Have you thought about your closing attorney? I have an excellent one that I've worked with before."* This next statement is used whether they have their own or they're ok with using yours...
  - *"I want to make sure they can accommodate your planned closing date. When is the soonest you'll want to close?"*

- *"Based on what I've seen it looks like we'll have to do the following items during the Due Diligence Period. I'll contact my providers of service to make sure they can accommodate your time-frame."*

Notice that with most of these statements I did not ask for the buyer's permission or their buy-in, I merely assumed that we needed to do this. If they don't stop me, then we're walking the trail together and getting closer to writing the offer. If they object, I know there is something blocking the trail.

Practice your closing techniques

Practice writing out a couple of closing style questions/statements given the following scenario...

> Sally and Mike are moving to town. They plan to buy and are interested in 3 BR 2 BA home near Lake Norman so they can occasionally use the lake for boating. You believe the home you're showing them is close to fulfilling their needs.

154

I'll give you one to help you get started...

> *"So Mike and Sally, the lake is great for boating. I know a couple of boat winterizing providers. I'll give them a call to see what they charge and if they have any slots available."*

Ok, one more...

> *"Mike, with your permission, I'll contact the HOA to be sure your can store your boat in the driveway."*

And one more...

> *"Sally I understand your concern regarding not having a place to store your boat. I've arranged for us to talk with LKN Boat Storage. Should they be able to accommodate your boat storage needs do you see this home working for you?*

Write out a few closing technique phrases that work for you...

_____

_____

_____

_____

_____

_____

_____

_____

I'm partial to the assumptive close but all of these closing techniques are effective in assisting the seller and buyer in making their decision. I want to stress that we are not using these techniques to "sell" – let's leave that to the used car salesmen we see in the movies – quite the contrary, these techniques are used to check in with the buyer and seller, to see where they are in their decision making process and to occasionally give them a gentle push so they can spread their wings and fly.

Of course, these techniques can be mixed and matched as needed. For example, if you are discussing buyer agency with a prospective buyer you could say something like, *"Mr. Buyer I assume you've already thought about the importance of having an agent represent your needs. Let me talk about the fiduciary duties I would have as your agent."*

As an astute reader I'm sure you immediately picked up on the assumptive close and complimentary close combination. (Oops, I did it again.)

Practice your closing techniques until you begin to feel them coming out in regular conversations. The more comfortable you are the more natural they will sound. You want to get to the point where you find yourself closing without even knowing it. But again, I want to remind you these are not slick strategies to sucker a buyer into buying or a seller into selling, they are conversational tools to help you uncover and better understand your client's housing wants and needs. Do not shy away from them or you could find yourself continually frustrated trying to understand why the buyer doesn't like the homes you are viewing and why sellers aren't interested in hiring you.

I also encourage you to grab a fellow agent in your office and practice various role play closing techniques. Sure it will seem strange and you'll probably feel awkward at first but isn't that the point? Wouldn't you rather feel awkward in front of your friend/fellow agent instead of a prospective client? The whole point of role playing is to work through the awkwardness so when it counts you sound and act naturally.

⚡ Role play your closing techniques, listing and buyer presentations, and explaining the Working with Real Estate Agents Brochure once per week. This is a critical part of your professional development.

Trail Log:

_____

_____

_____

_____

_____

_____

_____

_____

_____

_____

_____

_____

_____

_____

_____

_____

_____

_____

_____

_____

_____

_____

_____

_____

_____

_____

_____

_____

_____

_____

_____

_____

_____

Chapter 14: Successfully reaching the Northern Terminus OR closing the transaction.

Interspersed within this chapter are comments from Samantha H. Terres, PLLC Attorney at Law. I hold Samantha in the highest regard and I have relied on her advice and counsel for many years. She has always provided me clear and succinct answers to my questions (even if I didn't want to hear them). Samantha's comments are indented and in quotes.

The closing

The closing (as it is commonly known) is really the settlement meeting; a meeting in which the buyer and seller "settle up" and all documentation is reviewed and signed. This is also where, if you are not careful, tempers can flair. The best course of action for the agent is to treat the closing as a business transaction and check your emotions at the door (better yet, read about green apples in Chapter 15). Two agents having a spat over an issue, no matter how critical or trivial, will simply inflame an already emotionally charged meeting. Recognize that the buyers and sellers are mentally, emotionally, and physically exhausted on the day of closing and may be running on very little sleep. One of the best things an agent can do to assure a smooth closing is to remain calm, to smile, and to offer assurances that everything will be addressed regardless of how difficult the closing may be.

> "Complete the intake information checklists that are sent to you and return them promptly. If you don't know the answer and can't find out for whatever reason, don't just leave something blank. Address it even if it is only to say that you don't know or can't find the answer, or the issue is 'N/A' the main point is to return these checklists promptly.
>
> The agent's role: BE A GOOD EXAMPLE/KEEP THE PEACE. Corny I know, but I have found that clients take on the persona of their Realtors. Try to keep the peace as much as possible. Tempers flare frequently and some

Realtors fan the flames by inserting their own inflammatory opinions about the other agent, attorney, other party, etc... Try to remember that we are all on the same team working toward a successful closing, and things will go more smoothly if we try to remain calm. Your clients are most likely going to follow your lead, so lead by appropriate (calm) example."

Samantha H. Terres, PLLC Attorney at Law

Scheduling the closing

It is important that the agent(s) coordinate the settlement date with the lender. For example, if the agent schedules closing 30 days out from the day of contract without checking with the lender, that agent may create a situation where the lender cannot accommodate the settlement date or may be rushed to provide the loan to meet that date. Putting the lender in this position may very well cause mistakes to occur. Coordinate your settlement date with all service providers before contract!

"It is best to schedule closings as follows:
Tuesday through Thursday in the morning. Recognize that many attorneys bundle up their closings for the day and use runners to go to the Register of Deeds. Closing in the afternoon may result in the deed not being recorded until the next day.

Courier/Recordation/Release of Funds. Most attorneys use courier services for recordation. Most of the couriers pick up for more than one law firm and they are contract employees who are not under our direct and immediate control. Because of this, we cannot tell you exactly at what moment the checks will be ready. There could be traffic issues, long lines to update the title search, long lines to record the documents, computers to update, the title can be down, etc.

Please exercise some common sense in this regard

because if you think about it, there are too many factors to render a specific time frame for checks to be made available. We can estimate as much as possible but it will not be an "exact science."

Because the interim interest buyers have to pay at closing is less at the end of the month, attorneys tend to see an increase in the number of closings. If at all possible, avoid end-of-the-month closings so that the attorney and paralegals are not rushed. It is important to note that closing at the end of the month does not save the buyer money. If the buyer closes at the end of the month, their next full mortgage payment will be due sooner than if they had closed toward the beginning of the month but paid interim interest. There is no such thing as a free lunch, and the buyer will pay all that is owed to the bank.

Note that if you schedule a closing close to a holiday in which government offices will be closed, the deed may not be recorded in a timely fashion.

Time frame. Let the client know in advance the attorney's time frame for closing (i.e. 90 minutes, etc.) so that he will understand that he doesn't have the entire day. Along those lines, if a client tells you they are a reader (i.e. reading every word of every document), please let the closing attorney know so that they can, to the greatest extent possible, make arrangements with the Lender to get a copy of the package to the Buyer in advance of closing.

Be on time. Please have your clients at closing on time. Most of us have closings back-to-back and allow anywhere from 30 minutes to an hour for each one, so we can't accommodate a large closing package, or worse yet, a first and second combo loan structure, etc., when

160

clients arrive late because they are tired from moving or didn't want to get up that early or couldn't find the office... you fill in the blank. We may have to move the closing altogether because we literally have nowhere to put it and most of us are not going to inconvenience an on-time client for the sake of one who disrespected everyone else's time schedule. Along these same lines, if you aren't accompanying your client in the same car or having them follow you, make sure they have good directions so that isn't one of his excuses for being late. In addressing this issue, please understand that I am not talking about traffic, accidents on freeways, etc..."

Samantha H. Terres, PLLC Attorney at Law

While representing a seller, this author witnessed an attorney speak to his buyer client (the buyer hired the attorney) in an abrupt and, in this author's opinion, unprofessional manner. While the buyer was attempting to read the first document, the attorney literally snatched the document out of the buyer's hands and barked, *"You want the money?!?"* *"Yes"* said the buyer, *"Then sign!"* replied the attorney. Rude, yes, and the buyer (or worse, the buyer's agent) had selected the attorney. Get to know the attorney's style before you enlist their help in closing the transaction.

What?!? You're not going to be at closing?

You owe fiduciary duties to either the buyer or seller. As such, it is your responsibility to attend closing. In addition, it is a requirement of North Carolina Real Estate Commission rules that agents attend closing. Do not shirk this responsibility even if the buyer and seller say you don't need to come. After all, why wouldn't they want you at closing?

AWOL clients

If one or more of your clients is unable to attend closing, inform the attorney as soon as possible. There are options available to the attorney but they all take time to coordinate. The attorney can execute a POA

(Power of Attorney) (see below notes regarding POA), mail away the necessary documents, or allow the party to come in early or late if necessary, but if you inform them at the settlement meeting or the day of closing it may be too late to execute a POA and certainly a mail away will not work. If you've scheduled closing at the end of the month the attorney may not be able to accommodate you at all on that day resulting in your closing slipping a day or more. As a result the recordation of the deed will also be delayed. This is not a minor issue because it is the recordation of the deed that proves ownership and allows checks to be disbursed (including your commission). Not to mention the buyer's obvious and justified frustration in not being able to occupy the home on the day they had intended to.

POAs may not be used without specific permission of the lender; which could further delay your closing. In addition POAs expire so be sure your client can produce a current POA. And finally, you must produce an original POA for the attorney to record the deed. The Register of Deeds will require this.

> "Let the attorney know as soon as possible if there is a spouse who is not on the Contract. Everyone remembers the phrase "One to buy, two to sell," but what Realtors don't always remember is that some Lenders have their own internal policies requiring the non-borrowing spouse to execute certain documents regardless of whether he or she is on the loan or even on the Title. In that same vein, if the Buyer or Seller has a relevant document such as their own POA, a Quit-Claim Deed to convey marital interest, Pre-Nuptial, Free Trader Agreement, etc... please do not wait until closing to bring it to the attention of the attorney. Problems that may arise include: The document is not in a format approved by the Lender or Title Insurance Company, or the document has not been recorded, or has not been recorded in the correct county. We then have to collect for recording fees and add that to the HUD-1. In other words, do not practice law by assuming the document

162

your client has is sufficient. Let the closing attorney
make that call."

Samantha H. Terres, PLLC Attorney at Law

Remember that attorneys now require proof of identification before
closing to assure the girlfriend or boyfriend is not posing as the spouse
(yes that has happened). Be sure all parties have a valid driver's license
or other official document to prove they are who they say they are.

Show me the money!

One of the biggest issues that can arise at closing and one that can send
tempers flying has nothing to do with the buyer and seller. It comes from
agents disputing their commission amounts. It is critical that you fully
understand your compensation prior to closing. Closing is neither the
time nor the place to discover you will not be receiving the commission
amount you expected.

When you check the HUD-1 for your commission, don't embarrass
yourself and the attorney by stating the commission amount is, *"five
thousand dollars too little"* because your firm is holding the earnest
money that will be applied to the commission but you didn't realize that.
A firm may transfer the earnest money to the attorney or it may hold the
money and use it to pay a portion of the commission; as such, the
attorney may indicate a smaller amount of commission collected at
closing but a debit to the seller for the earnest money amount.

Funding closing

> **"Certified funds:** Please make sure to tell clients that
> they need a certified check, wire, etc., for payment of
> their closing costs. We try to communicate this as well,
> but Realtors have much more pre-closing contact with
> the clients than we do. FYI: North Carolina Statute
> allows attorneys to take up to $5,000 in the form of a
> personal check, but most impose their own internal
> limit...usually $500.00. Check with the preferred closing
> attorney about his or her structure in this regard.

Timing of the certified funds: Also related to this topic, clients will say 'I'm late because I had to go get my check.' Don't assume that is the order in which the attorney wants them to do it, i.e. most of us would prefer an on-time closing and getting the check right after the closing is concluded. This has become more of an issue because of lenders not getting us packages until right before the closing (not enough time to get HUD-1's to everyone in advance*)*.

Wiring funds: Listing agents should suggest that Sellers get wiring instructions to the closing attorney for the wiring of their proceeds. Note that the attorney may charge a nominal fee. The reason for this is that Sellers usually need their proceeds as promptly as possible to roll into their own purchase. Banks sometimes place a 3-10 day hold on a lawyers trust account check, so the funds will be more immediately available to the Seller if it is wired to her."

Samantha H. Terres, PLLC Attorney at Law

Also note that many attorneys prefer that buyers wire funds. This can speed up the transaction. With the advent of high-quality printers, banks frequently place holds on money orders in the event that the money order is fraudulent. Check with the attorney at the time of contract to determine the best course of action regarding monies.

Remind buyers and sellers to bring their checkbooks to cover unexpected fees. Checkbooks can and do get packed away and nothing can create problems and flare tempers at closing like a missing checkbook!

Checking the HUD-1 for accuracy

The North Carolina Real Estate Commission holds the agents responsible for the accuracy of the HUD-1. It is critical that you know how to calculate Pro-Rated Taxes, Interim Interest, and Excise tax.

Further, you should clearly understand all of the expenses that were incurred during the transaction to assure they are accurately reflected on the HUD-1 as a proper charge or POC (Paid Outside Closing).

> "Check the HUD-1 for accuracy. Check fax/e-mail before continually calling for a HUD-1. You'd be surprised how many Realtors will call 'ad nauseum' and we have already sent the HUD-1 to the number/e-mail address that they told us to send it to, but the Realtor never bothered to look before calling (again). This drives the paralegals crazier than anything. Also, along these same lines, if we say, 'I'll call you as soon as we have a package', we mean that. Calling repeatedly is doing nothing but preventing the paralegals from doing their jobs. Also, after asking the paralegals for the HUD-1, be sure to review it. Common issue: we assume 6% commission unless told otherwise or stated clearly to the contrary on checklist, contract, etc. You would be surprised how many Realtors will actually sit through the closing, pick up their checks and then we get a call post-disbursement, from the Realtors' broker saying the check we passed out to them is incorrect because of the commission."
>
> *Samantha H. Terres, PLLC Attorney at Law*

It is important for all agents to know that the North Carolina Real Estate Commission holds the agent responsible for the accuracy of the HUD-1. It is imperative that you review the HUD-1 when the closing begins (and if provided a copy prior to closing to review that copy in the event there are changes). The HUD-1 is usually the first document to be reviewed at the settlement meeting.

You curled up in a ball but the bear still attacked OR in spite of everything, there is still a problem at closing

Of course your objective is to make sure you have done everything you can to assure closing goes smoothly, but in spite of our best efforts, some closings will experience problems. If we only knew what caused problem closings, maybe we could avoid them. Fortunately you're reading this book. Here are the primary reasons closings do not go smoothly:

- An invoice payment is on the HUD-1 but the buyer already paid the invoice.

- Invoice(s) payments not reflected on the HUD-1 because the attorney did not receive the invoice from the agent or did not place the invoice amount on the HUD-1. It is important to bring copies of all invoices to closing to check the HUD-1 for accuracy and/or show proof of payment. Be sure to have the vendor providing service reflect that payment was or was not made so there is no question on the day of closing.

- Tax pro-rations and interest charges that are incorrect because closing moved to a different day.

- The agent's commission amount is in error or misunderstood.

- If the seller is contributing to the buyer's closing costs, be sure the amount of contribution is accurately reflected on the HUD-1.

- Agent bonuses paid to any party of the transaction must be accurately reflected on the HUD-1, must be approved by the lender, and must be approved by the client.

- The lender is delayed in getting the seller's loan payoff or buyer's loan package to the attorney. This can occur for a myriad of reasons but be sure you ask the attorney's paralegal if they have received the loan packages and if there is anything you can do to help. Several years ago while waiting for closing to begin I was informed that the lender had not delivered the loan package. They happened to be across town so I literally drove to the lenders office and picked up the loan package. They were surprised and, I must say, none too pleased to see me but you have to do whatever it takes to assure closing occurs, your clients are counting on it.

- The buyer is running late because they did not get to the bank to pick up their certified check. It is better they hurry to closing and pick up the check later. This would result in a "dry-closing" in which no monies are received but that can be easily corrected by the buyer going to the bank after closing.

- Misunderstanding of who is paying for what. Where possible, always review the HUD-1 with your client the day before closing. It may only be a preliminary HUD-1 but it will be very close to the final numbers. In one particularly contentious closing the buyers started arguing with my seller clients over thirty five dollars that the buyer's agent had failed to inform them was a buyer expense. I finally had to stand up and look Mr. Buyer in the eyes and say, *"This is not negotiable."* he was a "Tank" and I had to meet force with force. He backed down and the rest of closing went well. Had his agent informed him of this legitimate buyer expense prior to closing he could have vented his frustrations then.

  Remember that RESPA (Real Estate Settlement Procedures Act) only requires the HUD-1 to be provided to clients 24 hours prior to closing IF it is available. Most likely though the attorney will provide a preliminary HUD-1.

- The buyer or listing agent does not attend closing and the stand-in agent has not been briefed. Need I say more about this?

- Closing is at the end of the month on a Friday toward the end of the day. The attorney is rushed, the deed won't be recorded, the buyer will want the keys and the seller won't (and shouldn't) give them to the buyer. End of month, end of day closings are rarely smooth. Where possible avoid them like the plague!

- The walk-thru does not go well. It can be difficult to avoid this problem because of last minute damage caused by the seller's move, and/or the debris and garbage left behind by the seller or their failure to fulfill the terms of the contract regarding personal property and/or fixtures. My only advice is to be sure all parties are crystal clear as to their obligations under the contract. If you are the buyer's agent, identify personal property (make, model, and s/n) that is to remain and be sure you have clearly identified what repairs are to be made (see Chapter 20 "Repair request list"). If you have time prior to closing, strongly encourage the buyer to re-inspect the repaired items. Most inspectors will come back out for a reduced fee to inspect only the repaired items. If you are the listing agent, make sure the seller clearly understands they are not to play games regarding repairs. In other words, they must perform the repairs in a good and workman like manner – duct tape covering a hole in a leaking gutter which is then pained over to hide it is not a repair done in a good and workman like manner (I have a Realtor friend who did that on her own home). Also warn the seller that if they leave garbage and debris behind they are potentially in breach of contract and the buyer could walk from the contract.

- Of course there is the "who could have guessed that problem" closing. At one particularly long closing, the national wire service company's computers were down. This backed up the transfer of money for hundreds of thousands of transactions across the country. Our closing was scheduled for 9:00 AM and was finally completed it at 5:30 PM, a very long day indeed. All you can do is smile and eat lunch – which is what we did.

Steps you can take in the event of a problem with closing

Remain calm: This sounds obvious, but you have to constantly remind yourself that the problem should be resolved, but whether it is or is not, becoming emotional will not help the situation.

Smile: Laugh it off if you must! It will help you remain calm and help others keep things in perspective. Remember you made it this far so the odds are you will close even if you are a bit bruised and battered.

Do not raise your voice: Yelling is best left for running off an angry bear (or so I'm told). I have found that our clients take on our personalities. If we are calm, they tend to stay calm but if we get upset they are right there with us. Be careful what personality you are projecting.

Be sensitive to your party's needs:

- Is he or she hungry? Is it close to lunch time? A quick lunch while the attorney attempts to resolve the problem can do wonders for a smooth closing.
- Are the children becoming restless and agitated? Since you've been working with this buyer/seller for a period of time, you probably have a good idea what things interest the youngest members of this family. If possible, plan to have those items on hand for closing. I used to work with an agent who kept toys in the trunk of her car. They entertained the children during showings and at closings.
- Are there medical issues or prescription drug issues the buyer and seller need to be addressing but in the heat of the moment have forgotten? (i.e. a diabetic with low blood sugar).

Clearly define the problem and get agreement from all parties on how to resolve it. Avoid making broad sweeping general statements and certainly avoid making comparisons to other closings (i.e. *"When I worked with another attorney I never had this problem..."*) stay focused on the very specific issue and, if there are more than one, deal with them one at a time. This will keep the problem, or problems, from expanding into imaginary apocalyptic proportions; which they are prone to do but which they are not. I promise you it is never as bad as it appears. Here is a piece of advice I received several years ago from an experienced agent, *"Don't make the problem bigger than it has to be."* Brilliant!

Recognize that the attorney and paralegals are doing everything they can to assist you with the closing. Hounding them and demanding answers where none may exist will only exacerbate the situation.

169

Do not point fingers at the other agent. Even if the problem is the other agent's fault, pointing fingers will simply add fuel to an already emotionally charged fire. Any issues you have with the other agent should be discussed post-closing where cooler heads can prevail.

Do not interject yourself into the buyer's and seller's transaction. Remember the last time you were at the doctor and the nurse said, *"We need to take our shot."* Ok, they probably haven't said that in a long time but they used to and we didn't feel good about it because we weren't doing anything, you were or I was taking the shot! The same can be said for real estate transactions. It is not *our* closing or *our* offer. It is the buyers and sellers offer and closing. We often use the words *we* and *our* when talking about *their* transaction. To remain objective and calm, it is important that you avoid becoming emotionally wrapped up in the home sale and purchase. Avoid saying, *"we would like the following repairs"* or *"our offer is contingent upon_____."* By doing so, I believe you lose sight of who the buyer and seller are and thus it is more difficult to stay calm.

Good Fund Settlement Act

Essentially the Good Funds Settlement Act states that no funds may be disbursed from the attorney until the deed has been properly recorded and all monies have cleared their respective banks. What this means to you is you will not receive your commission check and if you represent the seller, they will not receive their funds until the Deed for the buyer has been recorded at the Register of Deeds. If your seller has a subsequent closing to purchase their home and there is a problem recording the Deed from the sale of their home, the seller's closing as the buyer will most likely be delayed or will be conducted as a dry closing (a dry closing is one in which no funds are provided but the documents are signed).

Good Funds Settlement Act: General Statute "§ 45A-4. Duty of settlement agent. The settlement agent shall cause recordation of the deed, if any, the deed of trust or mortgage, or other loan documents required to be recorded at settlement. The settlement agent shall not disburse any of the closing funds prior to the recordation of any deeds or loan documents required to be filed by the lender, if applicable, and verification that the closing funds used to fund disbursement are deposited in the settlement agent's trust or escrow account in one or more forms prescribed by this Chapter.

Trail Log:

Chapter 15: All trails lead somewhere OR other ideas to help you grow your business.

When I first came to this business I worked alongside a brand new agent who had been a housewife her entire life. I'm sure she worked around her home but she had no children, she had never had a paying job, and by her own admission, no jobs skills and certainly no skills in the field of sales. She is still in the real estate business today and continues to do quite well. How you ask? She had and has a very wealthy husband who funded her business from the start. Within a month of starting her career, she had hired a full time administrative assistant, she splashed advertisements everywhere, she bought a full size Xerox® copier and the latest electronic equipment needed to grow her business. Oh and a new BMW® to drive buyers around. Was I jealous? Would you be? But I also recognized then, as I do now, that we don't all have that advantage. If you are in the position to throw money at your business then I expect you will do very well but if you are like the vast majority of new agents, you will want to trade your time and efforts for your lack of money and/or smart frugality.

At least thirteen alternative low or no cost ways to boost your business

1. Join your neighborhood HOA board and get involved with your neighborhood.

2. If you have children, get involved with their school.

3. Volunteer at your church or local community center.

4. Offer to conduct a Short Sale and/or foreclosure seminar at your local church. Ask a local lender to assist you and help defer the costs for donuts (they will come for the donuts).

5. Go sit at coffee houses with your name tag on and business cards on the table. Coffee houses have become the new home office and office-office for that matter.
    - Always carry a business card in a place where you can quickly grab it (men your shirt's breast pocket works nicely, ladies wherever you can quickly get your hands on one). Often times the difference between smoothly providing your card and creating an awkward moment is the speed with which you can retrieve your business card. I like to play a game with myself and keep three business cards in my breast pocket with the goal of handing them out by the end of the day.

    - If you prefer, flip-flop this game and see if you can collect three business cards. This can be very beneficial because you now have a new prospect to follow up with and add to your contact database.

6. If you like to walk in your neighborhood wear your name tag and carry business cards. Plan to meet and greet people instead of just nodding at them as you walk by. If you walk frequently you'll most likely see the same people and soon you'll enjoy stopping to chat with them.

7. Visit local businesses, find the owner and strike up a conversation. Have a brief conversation as follows, *"Hi, I'm glad to meet you. You know from one business owner to another, I'm always curious about the issues we deal with. I'm hoping business is going well for you but what do you find to be your biggest issue?"* If they say they can't keep up with the bookkeeping and you happen to know an excellent, but out of work bookkeeper... Well you just might have a match made in heaven. Further, by asking this question you:
    - Have an opportunity to help another small business owner solve a problem.

- Have a reason to contact someone else who may be able to help that business owner solve their problem, thus helping two people.
- Create a reason to follow up with both parties to see if the problem was solved.
- Place both individuals in the position of owing you one and at a minimum you have established yourself as someone who adds value to the relationship.

I refer to this as servant leadership. Serving others naturally results in a benefit to you personally and professionally.

8. There are Pampered Chef® parties, Tupperware® parties, gold buying parties, etc… Host one or more of these company's parties and be that servant leader.

9. Join a networking group or start your own. If you do, be active and give more than you get. After all, there's no such thing as a free lunch.

10. Create an auto-email drip campaign. These are emails that automatically go out on a regular schedule without you having to do anything. Google "auto-email drip providers". Review Appendix E for useful resources.

11. Answer questions and build a profile at Zillow.com and Trulia.com.

12. Write a home buying field guide – and to answer your question, yes, you may "steal" the ideas you've garnered from this book – and share them with your friends and family. Further, ask them to distribute your guide to their friends and families.

13. Record internet videos and/or podcasts.

Make a list of your low cost or no cost marketing ideas:

Chapter 16: Choosing the wrong trail OR real estate agents biggest mistakes.

Agent mistake #1: Answering your own question

In my opinion, one of the biggest mistakes you can make is answering your own question. If you ask the seller, *"why is commission an issue?"* and then you say, *"Is it because you don't think I'm worth it?"* you have just answered the question for them. Even if it's not the true answer, you just gave the seller an easy out because they can now say, *"Why yes, it is because I don't think you're worth it."* It's hard to argue your way out of a corner you just put yourself in.

The hardest but most effective way to understand sellers and buyers motivation can be summed up in one word – silence.

"But", you say, *"I can't take the silence. It's awkward."* It is awkward, that's why you want to do it. You're not the only one in the room, it's very likely awkward for them too. Just relax, focus on your breathing, have a warm and caring smile on your face (one that says, *"I understand you're thinking about this so I'll give you all the time you need."*). One of two things is going to happen, either they will respond or the silence will go long enough that it becomes a game of who will speak first. The more you do this, the longer you can go but at some point you may have a person sitting across the table that likes to play the game of silence. If so, simply say in a humorous way *"Phew, I'm glad we cleared that up. Moving on, I was going to mention the (insert whatever you were planning to talk about next here)."* At this point if they let you move on, they may very well have resolved the issue in their own mind (they might just be an internal thinker) but if the issue is still out there, they'll bring you back to it and you can try again.

↑ Ask your question and then be quiet.

Agent mistake #2: Not asking for the order

As we discussed earlier, why would you lay a trail map out, pack your gear, tame the bears blocking your way, and then not ask the seller to walk the trail with you?

How do we ask for the order? Simple ASK FOR THE ORDER...
"Mr. and Mrs. Seller, I'm glad we've addressed your concerns and questions. I'm excited about working with you...

- *"... it takes only a few minutes to complete the paperwork."*

- *"...while I take a few pictures, will you complete the NC Residential property disclosure form?"*

- *"... I'll need about half an hour to complete the paperwork. Do we have time for that?"* (this technique works well with the "I'll get back to you" closing technique)

- *"... I believe we're on the same page. I'm ready to move forward with the paperwork."* (You say this as you are reaching for the listing agreement. This is a statement, not a question. You're not asking for permission, you are simply moving forward.)

- *"... to be sure I complete the listing agreement correctly, what personal property will remain, if any, and are you planning to take any fixtures?"*

- *"... as early as it is, I can have you on the MLS and on the internet tonight."*

- Or you could simply say. *"At this point we need to complete the listing agreement and other paperwork and then I can get started with the marketing of your property, is that ok with you?"*

Agent mistake #3: Closing on the phone

The purpose of the phone call is to set up the face-to-face meeting. Do not try to list the property or sell the property over the phone. Use the phone call to set up the appointment.

Agent mistake #4: Not establishing rapport

You must not go into a seller's home and tell them what they need to do to prepare their home for sale without first establishing rapport. Get to know them, understand their concerns first. As previously mentioned, I surely learned this one the hard way.

Agent mistake #5: Not actively listening

I am ashamed to admit this, but I am a terrible listener. I try, but if you talk for more than 10 seconds my mind begins to wander. Active listening is a skill that requires patience and practice. It is essential that you truly hear and understand what your prospects' and clients' are saying. Probably the best way to convince you is with an example:

Six months prior to writing this book I had a listing opportunity. I got the listing and a week into it the husband and I were chatting about insurance and I shared with him my views about the insurance industry and how they tend to look out for themselves. It's my opinion and I'm entitled to it. The only problem was this gentleman worked for the insurance industry. He was rather insulted with my characterization of the insurance industry. Looking back, I remembered him telling me this all important piece of information the day I met him. Sadly, I dismissed it only to rediscover that minor detail at the wrong time. They did not renew their listing, of which I was most relieved, when it expired and although there were various reasons given, I would hazard a guess that our backyard conversation contributed to the loss of the listing.

In another example, my wife and I sold our home. My name was on the sign and I was owner of record. I called an agent who had recently shown the home for feedback. I introduced myself as broker/owner, that clearly tells the other party that I own the property and I am a licensed real estate agent. Sadly, the agent did not actively listen. When prompted for feedback she stated that she couldn't imagine what the owner was thinking, *"Who would paint the children's bathroom that awful color?!?"* she pondered. First let me say that the awful color was the old Charlotte Hornets teal paint and my son loved it. Secondly, after I reiterated that I was the owner and I painted the bathroom there was 10 seconds of silence while the agent tried to recover; if you don't think 10 seconds is a long time, silently count to ten before answering your significant other's question and see how that goes. It certainly wasn't a huge gaff on that agent's part but actively listening would have avoided the situation all together.

Active listening skills start at the beginning of the conversation. If you've ever greeted someone with a **"Hi, how are you?"**, *"I'm fine, how are you?"*, **"Oh I'm very well, thanks for asking how are you?"**, *"Uh, well, as I mentioned, I'm fine."* You have just experienced someone (possibly you? and most likely me) not actively listening. The next time you say *"hello"* focus in on that person as if there is no one else in the room and nothing is more important than what they are about to say. And in case you're curious, I am working on my active listening skills and I have gotten better but it is a very hard trail indeed.

Here are a few active listening tips:
- Face the speaker and maintain eye contact.
- Mute or turn off electronic devices and put them out of sight.
- Pretend they are filling a bucket with information. Wait for them to finish before formulating your reply. This can be especially difficult if they are lodging a complaint. Remember though that the more information they give you, before you respond, the better your defense and/or response will be.
- Frequently nod your head and use verbal clues that you understand what they are saying.
- If you become lost in the conversation because you are confused or you lost focus, politely interrupt and ask for clarification.

Agent mistake #6: Not answering your phone or returning phone calls

I personally believe that you should not answer the phone while you are meeting with someone. My philosophy is that the person in front of you is more important than the person on the phone. Life is funny though, I was writing this chapter in a restaurant when a real estate agent I know came up to say hello. After exchanging pleasantries, I shared with him that I was writing a book and currently working on the chapter "Agents' Biggest Mistakes". Without hesitation he told me the biggest mistake he experiences are agents not answering their phones. With that, his phone rang (really, it did) and he excused himself. Ten minutes later he came back to finish our conversation and announced that the phone call he had just taken was from a seller asking him to come out to his house within the next hour or two to talk about listing his property. Now I admit, I found it a bit rude that he simply walked away from our conversation. Personally, I would not have answered the phone and I'm not convinced that had he not answered his phone he would have lost the opportunity for the listing appointment. But he does make a good point that we must answer our phones and return phone calls. Nothing irritates you, me, or real estate customers more than leaving a message and never receiving a phone call back. Not only is it bad business, it is just plain rude. Even if you have no answer or news to report, return that phone call. Here are four reasons you must return consumer's phone calls in a timely fashion:

1. By not returning their phone call, you tell them they are not important (just as you would feel if your call wasn't returned).

2. When you don't return phone calls, you don't just affect your business; you affect your entire firm's business because that consumer does not say *"[name] didn't return my call"*, they say *"[firm name] does not return calls"*.

3. I'm going to be blunt with you, if your BIC is getting calls from consumers to find out why they haven't received a return phone call from you, you aren't doing your job. Trust me; they will call your BIC if they don't hear from you.

4. At some point that consumer will move on to another agent and you will lose money, business, and any future referrals they may have provided!

Remember, in this business, silence is **not** golden. Make it a priority and part of your work ethic to return phone calls (as well as, emails and text messages) consistently and quickly.

Lest you think I am overstating this mistake, remember that year after year national surveys show real estate agent's lack of communication as the number one complaint by consumers; a complaint that is easily remedied by simply picking up the phone.

Agent mistake #7: Losing control of their calendar

You must control your calendar. You must keep only one calendar and you must block out personal and family time; if you don't you will be completely consumed by this business. When scheduling appointments make sure you identify two slots of time you can meet with the prospect prior to making the phone call, doing so will ensure you are in control of your calendar and they are not.

Agent mistake #8: Spending money unnecessarily or buying love

I often meet agent recruits and customers at coffee houses and restaurants. Sometimes I buy, but if I'm not careful I will spend an enormous amount of money unnecessarily. If you are meeting a friend, do you normally buy? Do they normally buy or do you go Dutch treat? Don't change the rules simply because you'll be talking about what you do for a living. I'm not saying you should never buy, but I think you need to be careful about taking the, "I'm buying" attitude into every meeting.

Agent mistake #9: Buying listings

We have already discussed taking an overpriced listing but it bears repeating that if you knowingly take a listing that is overpriced or worse you encourage the seller to list high, thus buying the listing, you will surely suffer the consequences. Remember listings are not equivalent to collecting memorabilia, we are not trying to collect the whole set. We are, however, in the business of selling those listings and if you dare take an overpriced listing, the seller will hold you accountable when it doesn't sell and they will hold you accountable when there are no showings and should the seller miraculously go under contract, they will hold you accountable when the home doesn't appraise for the agreed to purchase price. Resist taking an overpriced listing just to put a sign in the yard... *You've been warned!*

Agent mistake #10: Spending your commission before the check clears

Here is the one thing I have learned that I hope you embrace from day one. Until the check clears, trust nothing! Do not spend your commission check before you actually receive the check and it clears. Closings fall apart, attorneys bounce checks, buyers disappear, and sellers have regrets and back out of the contract. There are hundreds of reasons a closing will not take place. Be wise and don't spend the money you don't have. Along these lines, be prudent with your marketing dollars. Budget your money and expect to get a return on your marketing dollars.

Agent mistake #11: Lack of tax planning

Be sure you set monies aside for taxes. I did not set money aside or pay quarterly taxes my first year in the business and I was, how shall I put this... morosely despondent (these two 25 cent words are courtesy of my Thesaurus) when I discovered how much I owed the IRS and the lack of savings to pay that bill. I survived but don't make the same mistake. You are an independent contractor which means the firm you are associated with will not withhold money for taxes. You will receive a gross amount and you MUST be disciplined to set money aside. How much? Talk to your CPA but I would encourage you to set no less than 25% aside. Further, you will most likely have to pay quarterly estimated taxes. If, like me, you are not good with tax returns and tax planning consider hiring a good CPA – one who specializes in small firms and independent contractors.

Because real estate agents are independent contractors and the industry is rife with opportunities to hide money from the IRS, our industry tends to be on their audit hit parade. Consider purchasing financial tracking software such as Quicken® and/or Quickbooks® to help you track your expenses, manage your money and prepare your tax return information.

Agent mistake #12: Poor buyer agent etiquette
This category involves several mistakes.

I think one of the biggest mistakes we make as agents is not providing feedback on the showings we schedule. When a listing agent requests feedback on a property you showed, please provide that feedback. Understand that the listing agent is being pressured by the seller to find out how your showing went. Offering no feedback puts that agent in an uncomfortable position and reflects poorly on our entire industry. If you've shown eight homes that day (which in my opinion are four too many) you may not remember that particular listing; if this is the case, simply notify the listing agent that you don't remember the listing. At least they can let the seller know that the listing must not have been terribly memorable.

You should preview listings (or at least conduct a drive-by) before showing them to your buyer. However, when you call to set up the showing, please clearly state that this is a preview so the seller's hopes are not dashed and they understand that you are reviewing their home as a possible showing candidate.

If you need to cancel a showing, please notify the listing agent or the showing representative such as a Centralized Showing Service. In my opinion with the advantages of cell phones, text messaging, and other forms of communication there is no excuse for not cancelling the showing. Please understand that the seller has spent time preparing the home; they may have had to rearrange their schedule and/or their children may have been dropped off at a neighbor's house (possibly inconveniencing the neighbor). It is unprofessional and, if I may say, just plain rude to not properly cancel a showing.

Agent mistake #13: Unwilling to say "I don't know"

Years ago I asked a listing agent, *"What is that pipe sticking out of the ground?"* (It was the fill line for the underground heating oil storage tank). Instead of properly answering, *"I don't know but I will find out."* she stated rather assuredly, *"I think it's for a clothes line."* The pipe was only a few feet from the house, no clothes line would have fit. Imagine if I had not done my own discovery and purchased the house based on her answer. I may have been saddled with the expense of cleaning up that underground storage tank and she may have had to saddle her horse and ride to Raleigh to explain to the NC Real Estate Commission why she had just committed negligent misrepresentation (Yes, I readily admit, this is the worst and certainly the corniest analogy in the entire book; although you are free to disagree.).

Maybe this one should be the number one agent mistake. I think as a new agent, we all feel like we have to have the answer to every question. I assure you, you don't and you won't ever have the answer to every question. Please get comfortable and become confident in saying, *"I don't know but I will find out."* You will protect yourself and you will better serve your clients.

Agent Mistake #14: Prospecting ends when you get busy

Forget what I said about #13 being the biggest mistake, because without a doubt this is the number one mistake agents make. I saved it for last though in hopes it will be the mistake you remember most. Prospecting for new clients is your number one priority. Nothing, and I do mean nothing, in this business is a higher priority. Having all the education, scripts, and dialogs will do you no good if you don't have clients; and you won't have clients if you don't prospect. How you prospect is up to you, but you must do it either manually and/or automatically. If we had a Real Estate Bible, the Ten Commandments would read:

1. *Thou shalt prospect.*
2. *Thou shalt prospect.*
3. *Thou shalt prospect.*
4. *Thou shalt prospect.*

5. *Thou shalt prospect.*
6. *Thou shalt prospect.*
7. *Thou shalt prospect.*
8. *Thou shalt prospect.*
9. *Thou shalt prospect.*
10. *Thou shalt perform other business related activities.*

As we get busy, prospecting tends to be one of the first things to fall away. I believe this is so because as necessary as it is, for many of us (I include myself), it is not the most enjoyable task. Of course, neither is flossing or shaving or emptying the garbage or cleaning up your dog's waste or emptying the cat's litter box or cleaning the toilet or pulling the dead raccoon from the crawlspace or pulling weeds or paying taxes, or, or, or (feel free to add your own)... the point is we do these things because we must and although we don't always enjoy them, we do them. Prospecting for new business is no different. In my opinion lack of prospecting is the number one reason agents fail. Strike that – regardless of my opinion – it *is* the number one reason agents fail. These agents may have a leg up when they first get into the business because their circle of influence is large and/or productive but once those initial leads are used up, then what?

If you can't or won't prospect every day (even – especially – when you are busy) then figure out a way to automate prospecting. It is not a matter of if, but when you will fall out of the business if you do not actively prospect.

What mistakes do you anticipate and what steps can you take to avoid them?

_____
_____
_____
_____
_____

Chapter 17: Your daily hike.

Now that you have properly supplied your hike with the right gear (as in you've practiced your 10 second elevator speech, rehearsed your listing and buyer presentations, studied your closing techniques, and reviewed the local housing market via the MLS) you're ready to jump headlong on to the Appalachian Trail. Hold on a moment; I think you'll agree that it doesn't make sense to attempt to hike the entire trail in one long hike. Nope, you will have to break it down into daily hikes with contingency plans along the way should one day's hike not go as well as planned.

Remember the story of Jennifer Pharr Davis? She completed the 2,175 mile AT hike faster than anyone ever has. She averaged 46.9 miles per day and trimmed 26 hours off the previous record. I guarantee she had the big goal of finishing her journey but just as importantly she had daily goals to help her stay on target.

Structuring your days and weeks

Only you know when you are the most productive, most tired, most irritable, and most friendly. Given that, it would be counter-productive for me to lay out your day. However, there are certain things you must do each day to assure you are working toward your goals and maintaining a balanced life. How and when you do them is up to you.

As I have mentioned more often than you probably wanted to know, I wear my emotions on my sleeve. And in case you're wondering, no my wife does not like it, but she handles it beautifully and I love her for that.

Why do I bear my soul like this? Because I want you to know that it is ok to sometimes ignore your email, text messages, voice mails, and phone calls. Sometimes the best thing you can do is take a nap, go for a walk or run, yell at the top of your lungs, punch a pillow or whatever you need to do to work through the place you are in. Avoid returning phone calls or emails or text messages when you are "in that place". Unless bleeding is involved, 99% of your daily issues can wait a few minutes, if not a few hours. Should you respond while you're hurting or angry or sad, the words you say cannot be taken back.

I am a Broker in Charge which means that I promise the NC RE Commission that I will directly and actively supervise provisional brokers. I take that responsibility very seriously but I also know that if they are calling me, I need to be in the best place I can be and if I am not... well that's why we have voice-mail.

If you're not in the right frame of mind to work your business, take the time necessary to get yourself there. Embrace all your feelings and emotions; they are yours and you have a right to them but recognize which ones you are experiencing and think before reacting to a ringing phone or email/text message. And for those of you under the age of 40, remember a ringing phone is merely a *suggestion* to answer it.

Scheduling the week
It is a good idea to spend the evening prior to the first day of your work week reviewing your upcoming week's calendar. This gives you a broad idea of pending meetings and to-do items and mentally prepares you to face the week. Spend five to 10 minutes reviewing your upcoming week's calendar so you have a clear picture of how the week will unfold.

Just as importantly, you must schedule at least one day per week as a rest/rejuvenate day. This business can and will chew you up and spit you out. It doesn't care who you are, where you are from, or how much stamina you have. It will win – you will lose – if you don't schedule at least one day per week as a rest/rejuvenate day. This is mandatory, so figure out what that day will be. Change your voice mail and your email auto-reply to be sure you don't get sucked back into business on your day off.

> Here is a suggested outgoing message... *"Hi this is _____ I am spending the day with my family. Therefore I will not be able to return your phone call today. I do not want to lose you as a client so please leave your name and number and I will return your call first thing in the morning. Thank you."* The point is to be clear that you are the kind of agent that strikes a balance

in your life. You also want to throw a little guilt their way so they simply won't find another agent.

There is only one exception for working on your rest/rejuvenate day and that is to attend a closing. This is the only time you should consider working on that day.

Communicating with the natives OR handling your voicemail and email

In the morning, your first task should be to update your outgoing voicemail message. If you use an e-mail auto-reply then update that too. Be sure callers know your schedule and when you are available to return phone calls.

If you say that you will return calls between 3 and 4 PM do it! No excuses. The number one complaint clients, customers, and other real estate agents consistently have is the lack of returned phone calls. Separate yourself from the crowd by returning all phone calls when you say you will – even if your answer is *"I don't know, but I will find out."*

Professionally handling voicemail and email:

- If you call someone and you receive their voicemail, please leave the reason you're calling so that they, in turn, can reply with an answer should they get your voicemail. Have you ever retrieved this message, *"Hi, this is (me), call me I have a question."* Sure you have, and weren't you a little curious about the specifics of that question?
- If you are returning a call with an answer, do not simply tell them you are returning their call. Leave the answer they were looking for.
- Check your voice mail regularly and keep in mind the age of the caller. The baby boom generation will wait four to six hours without having a coronary. The millennial generation will expect a much quicker response and they will more than likely use text messaging.

↑ Text messaging in North Carolina is considered oral communication, not written. If you are responding to a contract provision that requires it be in writing, do not use a text message.

I may be a bit of a curmudgeon but I would like you to consider that email is a great way to share information and is ideally suited to organize and maintain records of your conversations, but it is a terrible communicator. Please do not hide behind email. If it is an urgent matter, text or call; do not rely on email to provide timely information. Lest you think no agent would ever do that, read on…

An agent at our firm was recently put in a difficult predicament because a buyer agent emailed her an ultimatum with a four hour window to submit the seller's counter-offer by 5 PM, otherwise the buyer would withdraw their offer. Unfortunately this agent, through no fault of her own, was having trouble with email and did not receive the buyer agent's email, nor learn of its existence until 6 PM. The buyer's agent never called to confirm that our agent had received the email. In fact she did not text or tweet or send up a flare or even call out the cavalry. In fact, the buyer's agent made no attempt to see what was going on or why our agent had failed to respond. Do you think the buyer's agent hid behind her email and failed in her fiduciary duties to her client? I do.

I suppose you could argue that our agent had some responsibilities, and you would be right had she known of the existence of the email, but how can you expect another agent to guess that you've sent them an email. Be prudent and follow up with a phone call; particularly when the matter is urgent.

Spending the day at your campsite OR working from home

If you choose to work from home, here are some tips to help you convey a professional demeanor:

- Always dress as if you're going into an office, because you are… it just happens to be a few doors down from your bedroom. Clothes do make the person. Don't dismiss this and assume it applies to others. Do yourself a favor and try it a couple of times. Compare those days to the days you never got out of your morning sweats and see if it doesn't make a difference.

- Put something that makes you smile next to your phone to remind you to smile. If you have a picture of a favorite place put that there too. It will calm you when you look at it.

- I have found that if I wear my headset I do much better when I'm walking around instead of just sitting at my desk. My responses are quicker and sharper and I'm more in tune with the caller. Interestingly recent studies have shown that exercise is actually better for the brain than the body. Next time you're on the phone walk around.

- Never say *"I work from home."* Instead say *"I work from my home-office."* Or, *"I'm working from my home-office today."* Subtle yes, but it makes a big difference. One sounds a bit amateurish and the other sounds professional. I'll let you decide which is which.

- If you work for a small firm or a virtual office or you're the kind of agent who only goes into the office once a month because your mail box is stuffed with flyers that you will never read and the administrative staff has asked you to clean it out so it can be stuffed, yet again, with more flyers that you'll never read, don't imply you do not have an office. Simply say *"I work from my home office, our headquarters is in [name of city] but we have agents all over the [name of city] metro market."* (Of course only say this if it's true.)

Learning the call of the wild OR the need for daily conversations

Disclosure: Once you join a firm, they should provide guidance for generating business but no matter what firm you join, it all starts with daily conversations with your friends and family…

FORD (it doesn't mean Found On the Road Dead)

If you are struggling with what to say or how you will fill the daily conversations you need to have with your circle of influence, consider the FORD method.

The FORD methodology allows you to converse with almost anyone of any age. FORD assures that you control the conversation while gaining great insight into the other person's life.

You see, people love to talk about themselves, their family, their successes (and failures), their friends, etc…all you need to do is know how to direct the conversation. The next time you are in a conversation, cycle through these four words (Family, Occupation, Recreation, Dreams); if they talk about their children, cycle through the four words again while talking about their children. Of course you don't need to use these actual words, they are merely prompts to help you remember what to ask. In other words, you don't need to say, *"What are your son's dreams?"* The word dream is the prompt for you to ask *"So what are your son's plans?"*

 Tip: Carry a digital recorder or a notepad with you. If you are talking with someone at a party (and I hope you are, since you are in the business of creating relationships) about their potential housing needs or their interest in selling a home, you will want to take a moment to discreetly jot or record a few notes. They'll be impressed with your strong memory the next time you talk with them.

Just as importantly though remember the concept of First Substantial Contact and your responsibility to discuss the

Working with Real Estate Agents Brochure contents, or at a minimum to warn someone not to say anything they wouldn't want another party in a potential transaction to know about, is alive and well even at a party. Do not allow yourself to find out confidential information without first warning that party-goer it could be used against them in a transaction.

Prospecting for gold

Make a copy of this card and keep it with you...

> **3 – 2 – 1 Every day my goal is to accomplish...**
> - Three face-to-face contacts to share my 10 second elevator speech.
> - Two hand written notes/Emails
> - One break-bread meal
>
> 5 - 10 calls per day using the FORD methodology.
> (Family, Occupation, Recreation, Dreams)

Note: Leaving a message counts as a phone call, however, your goal should be actual conversations. And you don't necessarily have to include your 10 second elevator speech in the phone call but if it is appropriate, include it.

It is very important that you log your conversation immediately afterward!! No Exceptions. It is terribly embarrassing to follow up, only to have forgotten that their son was ill or their daughter had just won a big award.

This activity will result in 15 face-to-face meetings per week, five break-bread meals, and 10 hand-written notes plus up to 50 phone calls. Real estate is a numbers game and consistently working this lead generation system will result in listing and buyer opportunities.

However, you will also be successful if you don't use this method. That is, if you want it badly enough and you have the resources to last a very,

very, long time. The difference is you will limp along and make little progress growing your business. It is analogous to taking the highway VS a country lane. They'll both get you to the same destination but the highway will get you there a lot quicker. I suppose, however, that if you have unlimited savings and the patience of Job you will survive.

I recognize the discipline it takes to prospect every day. I know it isn't always fun and there are days you won't want to talk with anyone, or at least not talk to them about real estate. But you have to have a goal. You may not always make it but you must try. It is no different than being momentarily lost in the woods and walking from one tree to the next until you have found your way again. You must hold yourself accountable and realize that at the end of the day there is no paycheck waiting for you. Each day ask yourself this question: *"If I were my own employee would I have fired myself or given myself a raise?"* Strive to impress yourself and expect a raise every day.

Although I have discussed this before, I believe it bears repeating… regardless of how you develop your business, whether it is through phone calls, or blogging, or a method of your own choosing, you must do it consistently. Consistency is the life blood of this business. Take my advice, or don't, but realize that whatever you do, you must do it consistently and frequently.

If you prefer, here is another way to organize your day...

Task	Your Points	Desired Points
Lead generation is your number-one priority; it should consume most of your day and/or activities.		
1. Speak to no less than five people today (in person or on the phone). One point for each person as long as they know by the end of the conversation you are in real estate! Use the **FORD** methodology for conversation (ask about their Family, Occupation, Recreation/Relaxation and Dreams).		5
2. Email no less than five people today (I don't care what you say, just make sure they know you exist as a real estate agent available to help them).		2
3. Update your social media accounts with current topics (Twitter, Facebook, etc...).		2
4. Visit Trulia, Zillow, etc..., and answer no less than five questions.		2
5. Write three thank you cards, congratulatory, or simply a "hello" card to past clients, current clients, small business owners, service providers, family, friends etc....		3
6. Spend one hour in the **same** public place with the intent of		5

smiling, meeting people, handing out business cards, or simply putting a friendly face on. Go sit at a coffee house while you write your letters and put business cards on the table. Look up, smile and say "hello" to people. Be friendly! You get no points if you did not make contact with people or had a grumpy face.		
7. Work through your contact database and tick off what you did for each person so that by the end of 10 weeks, you have touched each of them in some way no less than five times.		1
8. Contact a provider of service. For example if you are working the foreclosure market, contact two lenders to generate opportunities.		3
9. Set up an appointment with a buyer or seller…		4
Your tasks directly applicable to lead generation…		4
Market education: Spend one to two hours educating yourself on your market, the MLS, chosen neighborhoods, etc…		4
Sharpening your saw is also important. What area have you decided to focus on? If you want to be a foreclosure expert then study a foreclosure article, read a book, review a website for one hour.		4

File management, maintenance, office organization (sure this is important but without leads, office organization is nothing but "feel good" busy work. That's why it only gets one point).		1
Your personal health is critical. One hour sharpening your own saw.		10
Total points		**50**

Remember, my goals are not your goals so feel free to modify this worksheet and the points awarded. Whatever you create though, be sure it pushes you and uses the SMART methodology (see Chapter Six) for goal setting, and it is primarily focused on lead generation.

The number of ways to generate business is as varied as real estate itself. If you don't like my suggestions, I won't be offended but find a way everyday to put yourself in front of the maximum number of people who can and will help you grow your business. Write down your ideas to consistently generate leads and keep it with you.

_____

_____

_____

_____

_____

_____

_____

_____

_____

_____

_____

_____

_____

Survival skills when calling people

I understand your concerns about calling people on the phone. I suggest the following tricks to help alleviate this and remember, the more you do it, the easier it gets.

- Create a carrot on a stick for yourself. I read a few years back about a broker who stripped naked when calling prospects. The article conveyed that he handed his clothes to his assistant (I presume through a partially closed door) and he would not get dressed until he had made all of his calls. If you decide to do this and you call me to tell me it is working, please don't tell me you're practicing it while we're talking and PLEASE do not use iPhone's Facetime.

- Stand up and walk around. It will give you energy and burn a few calories and you will be more creative because as mentioned, exercise is actually better for the mind than the body.

- Smile before you dial! This will help you relax. Laugh out loud if you must. I know this seems silly and we've heard it before, but that's because it works.

- If you're really freaked about dialing, do what I do, close your database, notebook, etc... and then dial the number. While the phone is ringing you'll be so busy getting everything back open and ready for the call, you'll forget about your nervousness (Caution: Remember who you're calling. It is very embarrassing to say, *"Now who am I calling?"* which I did once.).

- You could let them know right up front that this is a short business call. *"Hi _____, this is (me), do you have a couple of minutes? This is a brief business call. As you know I'm a real estate agent and I just wanted to remind you that I focus on _____. Should you know of anyone needing this service please let them know I'm available."* (Now at this point you could even have fun the first couple of times by saying, *"phew, I'm glad that's over with"*, but I would only do that with my closest friends and family.) During the rest of the phone call utilize the FORD technique and make the rest of the

197

conversation about them. **Keep the call to no more than five minutes** and wrap it up by saying, *"Bob, it's been great talking with you, thanks for updating me on what's been going on and for allowing me to share with you what I'm doing. I'll give you a call next week to touch base."*

In each of your follow up phone calls you should:

☎ Refer back to some tidbit in the previous conversation.

☎ Ask for a referral or at least remind them about your business and what you are trying to accomplish.

☎ Be sure they know, as best as possible, what you are looking for in a potential client. Think of it this way, if your friend called and said they were looking for a job because they had just been laid off but they couldn't tell you the type of job they were looking for, when they could start, what their salary requirements were, etc, etc… you would probably have a tough time helping them.

☎ Utilize the FORD conversation method.

Now this next step is very important: Immediately record your conversation in your database so that when you talk with them next, you'll remember what you talked about the last time. Trust me, when you call next week and remind them of some small tidbit from your previous conversation, they'll be impressed and they will appreciate that you actually listened to them.

I found out the hard way that if you get too detailed in your recollection of the previous conversation, they become a little suspicious. In one memorable conversation the person I was talking with was so impressed with my recall she asked, *"Are you reading from your notes?"* I admitted that I was but that I didn't have a great memory and our conversations were important to me. I still talk with her from time to time but I don't "recall" much from the previous conversation and I've never gotten a referral from her so I'm not sure if she was offended or not. With that said though, you still need to take notes because if you don't and you're talking to several people every day you will be hard pressed to recall

198

those conversations which can be even more embarrassing than remembering too much.

If you reach their voice mail, leave a message like the following:

"Hi Bob, this is _____. I hope you're well. I was just thinking it's been a while since I caught up with you" (or *"I was just thinking about our conversation last week – [reference the tidbit]"*).

Then say....

☎ *"There's been some interesting news in the world of real estate that I thought you would be interested in."* Or...

☎ *"I had a transaction last week that made me think of you."* Or...

☎ *"I wanted to update you about a recent sale in your neighborhood."* This can be powerful because it lets them know you're on top of your game and you're giving them useful information about their neighborhood.

Follow that up with, *"No need to call me back, I'll try again later."* This takes the pressure off them to return your phone call, but gives them the option should they desire to do so.

Here's the good news, phoning five people per day shouldn't take more than half an hour, and it is a half hour very well spent. I'm sure you did the math and you calculated that it works out to be only six minutes per call, but sit silently for six minutes and you'll get a sense of how long that really is. Eventually you will want to get to 10 or 15 calls per day, but five is very doable and will help you grow your business.

Planning a vacation?

Vacations are a critical way to stay fresh and enjoy life. Make sure, however, that you have an agent covering your business and be sure they have the time to adequately do so. Should a closing occur during your vacation recognize that an agent must be present to represent the client's needs. If you cannot attend closing please be sure to arrange for an agent (preferably your BIC) to attend the closing on your behalf. As hard as we try to attend every closing, there are, admittedly, times when we've had that plane ticket and hotel reservation for months and our closing got bumped right into the middle of our vacation. Don't drop the ball and tell your client you'll see them when you get back. Be sure you find someone to represent you.

One of the biggest mistakes I ever made early in my career involved the representation of a buyer purchasing new construction. I admit I did not know much about closing with builders and I was in the middle of a forest of listings and contracts. I called the builder and asked if I needed to be at closing (what do you think he said?) What happened next was not pretty. The commission amount my firm collected was $8,000. The buyer did not know my split with the firm, but they did know my firm collected that amount. Although Mrs. Buyer was reasonably understanding, Mr. Buyer could not believe I had collected $8,000 (remember he didn't know my split amount) and that I hadn't even bothered to show up for closing. Needless to say, I never got a return phone call after closing, nor did they respond to my customer survey, I never received a referral and honestly I never heard from them again despite my repeated tries; one and done is not how you want to grow your business. And it goes without saying that I was in clear violation of NC RE Commission rules regarding my fiduciary duties.

↑ Be sure you have coverage for your closings and all your other business. Also consider what you are asking the covering agent to do and work out fair compensation *before* leaving for your vacation.

For a more detailed discussion of your daily and weekly activities, see Appendix B

Trail Log:

_____

_____

_____

_____

_____

_____

_____

_____

_____

_____

_____

_____

_____

_____

_____

_____

_____

_____

_____

_____

_____

_____

_____

_____

_____

_____

_____

_____

_____

_____

_____

_____

_____

Chapter 18: It's raining again?!? OR staying motivated and dealing with the frustrations of this business.

If you were hiking the AT, here is something you would want to keep in mind... *"If it gets better – keep hiking. If it stays the same – keep hiking. If it gets worse – keep hiking, until you can get to a doctor."* These are the words of Jennifer Pharr Davis holder of the fastest thru-hike in AT history.

No matter how well your day goes – keep prospecting. In spite of how frustrating your week is –keep prospecting. No matter how unproductive the past month was– keep prospecting. However you define prospecting, do it consistently and regularly, and remember for every agent that falls out of this business, a new opportunity is created for the one who stayed in the business. Will you create an opportunity for someone else's business? I hope not. You have to have the financial means, of that there is no doubt, but just as importantly you have to have the mental and emotional perseverance to keep pushing; even if (especially if) others are telling you to find another line of work because, in their opinion, the real estate industry is dead.

We talked about your BIG WHY in Chapter One and I hope you took the time to at least think about the true reason you want to help others buy and sell real estate (if you haven't, consider doing it now). Your BIG WHY will help you tremendously when times are difficult and you feel like walking, if not running, away from this business. But there are other ways to stay motivated too.

Encouragement and motivational tips

Trying to stay motivated and encouraged in this business is, at times, very much like hiking the AT in wet, rainy, and miserable conditions. All you really want to do is find a nice, dry and warm hotel, and give up the hike. In this business, when the accolades from past clients are flowing in it is easy to be encouraged and when you have closing after closing it is easy to stay motivated. But when the conditions change it is very easy and even understandable to want to give up. Don't! Keep prospecting, keep finding new business opportunities and review these tips or create your own to help you stay motivated and encouraged. Just like the AT this business has many ups and downs and it is in the down moments that you need draw upon your encouragement and motivational first-aid kit. A serious hiker never goes into the woods without a rudimentary first-aid kit and you should not go into this business without one too. Here are some suggested items you should put in your kit.

Keep things on an even keel: In the eyes of your clients, you will either be the goat or the hero; there is no middle ground. You either helped the seller sell or the buyer buy or you didn't. Over the long term your goal is to be the hero more often than the goat. But remind yourself regularly not to be too prideful when you are the hero nor disgraced when you are the goat.

Further, you cannot get too high in the highs of this business and you can't get too low in the lows. Keep things within a reasonably narrow range of emotion. Just got your first big check? Congratulations but keep it in perspective. Just lost the largest client you ever had? I feel bad for you but keep it in perspective. As they say in football, *"pretend you've been there before"* or as my sister, a practicing Realtor, says *"fake it till you make it"*.

Read your BIG WHY regularly and post it around your home to remind yourself why you are in this line of work. Take a few minutes and close your eyes. Visualize yourself accomplishing your goals. See your BIG WHY becoming a reality. Embrace how good it makes you feel and the sense of accomplishment your successes bring.

Keep an encouragement folder. Whenever you receive positive affirming words from someone, place them in your encouragement folder. If you're having a particularly rough day, read these words of encouragement. You'll be pleasantly surprised.

To encourage others to give you words of encouragement create a customer satisfaction survey and give it to each of your clients. Be sure you get their permission to use their words in future publications. Make copies of these surveys and keep them in your encouragement folder.

What if you receive a poor survey? Well, you don't have to use their comments; in fact you don't even have to keep the survey. Have a "bad survey" ceremony and set the survey afire while chanting, *"I will strive to do better."* Assuming, of course, it was your error that caused a poor review. Otherwise chant *"The seller (or buyer) is a jerk"*.

Invite your friends over and have a "frustration sharing" party. Everyone gets an opportunity to share what frustrates them and why. Support and encourage one another. If the group is asked to help solve an issue, work together and find solutions. If a particular issue is resolved then celebrate your success; otherwise throw the frustration into the proverbial (or real) fire and bask in its burning glow. Maybe Frank Costanza from the Seinfeld TV show had it right when he celebrated his annual "Festivus for the Rest of us" in which the participants each went around the room and shared their criticisms and grievances from the past year. Of course I think Frank took particular delight in complaining about his wife and son, so you may want to set some rules.

Do less and sleep more. If you find yourself unmotivated or demoralized, it may be stemming from the fact that you are trying to do too much and you're not sleeping enough. Study after study continues to show the great importance of sleep. However, you don't need a study to tell you how important it is, virtually all living things sleep, so it obviously serves a vital purpose.

I hear you; you don't think you can do less or sleep more, but I encourage you to try. If you will let the dishes stay dirty for a night, or leave the clothes in the dryer until morning instead of folding them at midnight, or if you don't cut the grass quite as often, or even clean the house every Saturday you may just surprise yourself with a little more time for a good night's sleep. If you have young children and you put them to bed at 8 PM, kiss them goodnight and go to bed yourself.

Ignore the man behind the curtain: If you are like me, your mind is occasionally visited by a little man (or woman) that loves nothing more than to scatter negative thought-seeds here and there. Seeds like, *"You're not good enough."* or *"You can't do it."* or other ridiculous assertions to

204

that effect. Try as we might, it is difficult to banish that little creature, but we can remember that their thoughts are not our thoughts. Let them have their little tantrums and then go about your business. Acknowledge their existence and watch the ridiculous things they say scroll across your mind like the crawler at the bottom of a newscast. Thank them for their thoughts and then move on. In other words, by separating yourself from their thoughts you prevent that little person from planting a thought-seed that very often grows into the tree-of-doom.

Get a coaching buddy. Someone that will hold you accountable for the goals you have set for yourself but will not be all in your face if you drop the ball. A best friend or another agent may work well. I would avoid your immediate family and your BIC. Call your coach first thing in the morning and let them know of one specific, yet challenging goal you expect to accomplish that day. Ask them to follow up with you in the evening. In fact, I encourage you to share your goal with as many people as you can; tell everyone you know what you are trying to accomplish. The more people you tell, the more likely you are to have to give a status update when you bump into them at the grocery store. The more committed I became to this book, the more people I told; I was not going to allow myself to secretly fail.

When you are in a particularly good mood write yourself several upbeat congratulatory and encouraging notes and put them in an envelope that is stamped and self-addressed to you. Give them to someone else and ask them to occasionally mail you one of your notes. I will bet a lot of money your note will happen to show up in your mailbox just at the right time.

Your Motivational and Encouragement thoughts:

_____

_____

_____

_____

_____

Dealing with the frustrations of this business

As with all businesses, there are ups and downs, successes and failures, and daily frustrations. If you don't experience these things and you are successful, you should write a book! Only you know how best to deal with the slings and arrows hurled your way, but here are a few suggestions.

Stop taking vacations

Many people enjoy planning and taking long vacations. If you're not one of them read on... Here is the problem with vacations as I see it. First you have to plan that large vacation while you're trying to juggle your work and daily life (stress). Then you take the vacation, which is great, except for the lost luggage, flight delays, unplanned rainy weather, etc. (more stress). Cell phone calls, faxes, emails during the vacation (even more stress). And finally you return to a pile of built-up paper work, irate clients, fallen through contracts and missed opportunities (congratulations, you reached the peak of stress).

Of course I'm kidding about not taking vacations. In fact I encourage you to take more of them! Consider taking more frequent and shorter ones; maybe even spur of the moment mini-vacations. Connect with a trusted agent who you know will cover your work duties in a professional and diligent manner. Contact all of your clients and notify them of your plans to take a vacation – upon your return you can send your clients photos and blog about your adventures.

Things to bring on your vacation: fun stuff
Things not to bring: work stuff

Pretty simple huh? By taking shorter and more frequent vacations you really can leave the work stuff behind. You don't have to worry about checking in because two days in the mountains is not going to create the same buildup in work as two weeks in Hawaii.

I suggest, if affordable, that you buy a second cell phone with another number. One that you can use to call out but can only be called by those you give the number to. Do not install email on it and do not give the

206

number to your clients. Better yet, get a Google Voice phone number. It's free and you can give it to only those people you want calling you. Will you be stressed the first time you don't check into the office every hour? Yes, but you'll soon get used to that and you will be much more productive upon your return. You have to give yourself permission to truly be on vacation and engrossed by the experience. If you try to take a vacation while you are regularly checking email and returning client phone calls you will have the same experience as trying to watch two movies at the same time. You won't enjoy either one of them.

As a suggestion to transitioning into this type of vacation, stop reading the newspaper and other trade journals for a couple of days. Tune out all television news, change your radio station in your car and listen to a music genre you've never listened to before. About two years ago I changed the radio station and started listening to country music. It's now one of my favorite stations and when I'm blue, and they start singing about momma or prison or drinking or pick-up trucks, well I just can't help but tap my foot and smile. Visit YouTube and type in those words plus "David Allen Coe", grab the drink of your choice, sit back, and enjoy...

In addition to altering your electronic-media settings, consider taking a "staycation". Sit in your chair and do absolutely nothing for an hour or two. I don't want you to fall asleep. I really want you to just sit there and stare at the wall. You will be amazed how creative your mind will become. Remember, we are human beings and sometimes it's ok to just be.

I'm sure the idea of taking vacations and staycations may sound a bit like heresy. After all, we're told that as real estate agents we can never stop prospecting (Let's be honest, even I said that earlier, but that's also why I'm a big proponent of automating your prospecting.) and we can never stop working the business. We are told that we are like sharks that can never stop swimming lest they die. Here's a dirty little secret... there are several varieties of sharks that do sleep; they lie on the bottom of the ocean floor and doze away rather nicely, thank you very much, and they don't die, in fact they're probably better hunters for it.

Preparation steps:

- Discuss vacation coverage duties with a trusted agent and help each other out.
- If necessary agree to a referral fee or compensation package with that agent.
- Notify your clients of your vacation plans and who is covering.
- As best as possible, do not schedule your vacation on top of an upcoming closing. If that is unavoidable, talk to your BIC and client to be sure closing is handled properly.
- Go on vacation. Simple, isn't it?

Stop working out

As I look back on my life I was reasonably athletic when I was younger. I was certainly no Olympian but I could keep up with just about anybody. As I've gotten older and look in the mirror, I notice that I still have that same great shape; it's just not in the same places it used to be. So what happened? I've gotten older for one thing but I think the bigger issue is the way that I work out. When I was young I didn't work out, I was simply active and play was a big part of my life. As I aged I fit in working out and the routine tended to be the same. After a while that routine got boring and so, like millions of others, I quit. The workout industry is a multi-million dollar business exactly because we get bored with our routines and we are looking for the next one that is #1 easy and #2 never boring. In fact, they are so used to us becoming bored, they now design exercise equipment that can be folded up and slid under a bed where, presumably, they are utilized to a great extent by the monsters that live there.

Why not multi-task. Wear your name-tag and go play for a while. Take an hour or two during the day to walk around. Go visit a museum, go for a stroll in a park, or wander around the mall for awhile. As an added benefit, scientists have now confirmed that movement is actually better for the mind than it is for the body. You may even come up with the next great real estate idea while wandering the mall! If you work out now, vary your routine and try something new like yoga or Pilates, swimming, or weight-lifting. If you don't work out now, don't worry, simply start moving and be sure to wear your name tag and Realtor pin.

If, however, you've worked out in the past but those days seem distant and you would like to start again, consider this… I have a love/hate relationship with exercise. By that I mean I love how I feel when I finish, but I hate starting. If you choose to work out, I encourage you to do it in the morning. There are too many excuses that arise during the day to justify (rightly or wrongly) not working out in the evening. To start my morning routine, I turn off my mind. In other words, like a zombie, I go up the stairs and mindlessly start stretching and lifting weights. I don't allow myself to think about what I am about to do or how much I'm going to accomplish, I simply start and the next thing I know I'm finished. To me it is more important to go through the motions than it is to have an engaged and productive workout session. Remember, staying in the routine, regardless of the quality of your workout, is more important than the actual workout because by staying in your routine you will have more good days than bad. And let's face it, if you don't stay in your routine your workouts will be far and few between. If it's been awhile and you regularly kick yourself for not working out but you just can't see yourself starting again, simply go through the motions for a few days; you might be pleasantly surprised.

Stop calling your clients and dialing for dollars

Just as with your physical workouts, I suggest that if you find yourself unmotivated in wanting to prospect, you may be in a rut and you need to change your routine. Stop calling people for a week, instead visit them. Stop writing blogs or answering Zillow.com questions and instead host a seminar (by the way, if no one shows up, conduct your seminar anyway. It's good practice). Spend time at a local coffee shop and purposely reach out to strangers. Typically the same people show up time and again so make some new friends and expand your circle of influence while you work yourself out of your rut.

Give yourself permission to be miserable

Should you find yourself angry and frustrated with your real estate business, other real estate agents and/or your clients and customers, give yourself permission to be miserable. In other words, you have my permission and you should give yourself permission to occasionally sit on your pity-pot. Grab a piece of paper, a pen, and a quiet place to vent your frustrations. Stand in your empty house and scream at the top of your lungs. Grab your pillow and punch away. 99% of the time you have a right to your frustrations and you have to have a way to release them because I promise you they will come out; it is not a matter of if but when; so take control of the when. In Japan there are hotels that offer their patrons the opportunity to spend a few minutes in a room smashing plates, cups and other dishes to their hearts content. Now that is a very cool, albeit dangerous, way to vent your frustration. If a quick jaunt to Japan is not in the cards, find another way to vent your frustrations because, again, they will come out at the most inopportune time.

Breath control can also help you work through your frustrations and angers. I don't just mean breathe to live. I mean live to breathe. Focus on your breath. To learn more, read a book or take a class on relaxation breathing techniques – oh and wear your nametag to class.

Here is a pretty neat trick. If you are sitting at a particularly frustrating closing and you feel your blood pressure rising, stop for a moment and think about green apples. Studies have shown that merely thinking about green apples and the way they smell reduces blood pressure.

I love what I do. I love helping agents succeed. I love helping students obtain their real estate license and witnessing their ah-ha moments. I couldn't have asked for a more perfect, if not accidental, career choice but with that said, there are times when I would rather not talk to anybody; I'd rather stand in an empty room and yell at the top of my lungs. (Which I occasionally do from time to time. Scream therapy was popular back in the 80's but so too was disco and we all know how that worked out.) Or I would rather be stung by a bee rather than have to explain, yet again, that *"no the seller cannot take any fixtures with them unless they have been specifically excluded in the contract. Why can't they? Because the contract says they can't!"* and so it goes. I have found that when I give myself permission to be miserable I am more motivated and more productive when I do work.

The customer is not always right

I have many pet peeves and at the top of my list is the expression *"the customer is always right"*. Who says they are always right? In fact, they are often wrong. I believe it is more appropriate to say *"the customer is not always right, but they are always the customer"*. It is ok to be upset when a customer or client complains about something that is either not your fault or was beyond yours, or anyone's, control or was in fact the customer's fault. Give yourself permission to privately vent and refuse to swallow whatever grief they are trying to feed you. If it's your fault, own up to it and correct your mistake, but if it is not your fault, be respectful (they are the customer after all) but be clear as to who or what properly owns the problem and although you must treat the customer with respect, do not accept ownership of a problem you did not cause and do not say, *"I'm sorry"*. Every time you say, *"I'm sorry"* to someone, you have accepted the ownership of the problem. After all, if it wasn't your fault why are you saying you're sorry? It is perfectly acceptable to say, *"I am sorry for the problem you are experiencing and I will do what I can to help you resolve it."* Do be careful, though of making a generic *"I'm sorry"* statement in hopes that it will make your client or customer feel better; it won't and it won't solve the problem.

I often hear the following in class *"I'm sorry but I have a question"*. Why is that student sorry they have a question – particularly since they are paying for the class? I believe that we have become a society that equates the words *"I'm sorry"* with *"excuse me"*. They are not the same and should not be used interchangeably. Refrain from saying you are sorry unless you mean it. You will have more control of your business because you will not accept ownership of errors that are not your fault.

211

Trail Log:

Chapter 19: Somebody's got to help keep the trail open OR a few words about service providers in the real estate industry.

I think it is a very good idea to have a list of service providers at your ready. But it is just as important to get to know them. As good as you will be as a real estate agent, it is your providers of service that can make or break your transactions and your reputation. Just like the quality of your hiking shoes or camping gear enables you to complete your AT hike, poor equipment can cause you to fail regardless of the shape you are in.

Interview your BIC and other agents in your office. See if you can find service providers used by more than one agent. It's a good bet they provide quality service if more than one agent is using them. Be careful about statements like: *"my brother, sister, aunt, best friend..., is an inspector you should call them"*. They may be great or it may be nothing more than blood running thicker than water. Further, just because your firm offers an in-house lender or in-house attorney, it does not mean they are the best in town. I realize I'm going out on a limb here but if your BIC is putting pressure on you to use their in-house lender or attorney it may not be because they are the best at what they do, but because they are helping to defray some of the costs associated with keeping the firm's doors open. In my opinion, you should never be pressed to use any one particular service provider. You should be free to interview and recommend to your clients ones that you have vetted based on your conversations and experiences with them.

In general you should avoid giving only one service provider's name to your client/customer because the liability of providing just one name may put you in the position of being held accountable for that service provider's mistakes. By giving the consumer several choices within a category (i.e. more than one inspector, lender, surveyor, attorney, etc...) and letting the consumer choose, reduces the risk of being held accountable for mistakes made by the service provider. However, I must admit I have provided only one name in any given category for many

213

years because I know the service provider's work and I know they provide excellent service and I have never had a complaint. Further, it isn't always easy to find more than one provider of service in a particular category. I offer this advice as more of a warning for you to think carefully when choosing your team of providers and for you to understand the possible consequences of choosing just one. Talk with other agents in your office and/or your BIC to find out what service providers they recommend. In all cases be sure you provide a Professional Services Disclosure form to your client. In essence it is a CYA (Cover Your "behind") document but it also serves to clarify the various services needed in the transaction and whether the consumer chooses to have those services performed.

Take the time to get to know your service providers. Trust me they can make or break a transaction and you really need to understand how they operate, the amount of time they need to perform their work and their style of communication before you enlist their help with a particularly difficult transaction.

Working with inspectors

There are as many inspectors as there are problems with homes; mold/mildew inspectors, termite and other wood boring insect inspectors, mechanical/structural, septic/well, radon, lead, EFIS (Exterior Finishing System and more commonly referred to as Synthetic Stucco) siding inspectors. In general you will need at minimum a mechanical/structural inspector and a wood boring insect inspector but the need for an inspector depends on whether the home is on well/septic, the age of the home, and the components of the home among other factors. Further, depending on the buyer's comfort level they may want to inspect for items you've never thought of. Many years ago we never inspected for Radon but now it's common practice.

In general, inspectors should indicate whether an item is performing the function for which it is intended or it is not performing that function. They should avoid making predictions about the remaining life of an item; at times, though, I have witnessed them doing just that. For example, I was involved in a transaction in which the inspector indicated

214

the HVAC (Heating, Ventilating and Cooling system) was performing the function for which intended but in that inspector's opinion the system would need to be replaced within eight months. Not six months, or one year, but eight months. How he possibly knew that exact time frame is anyone's guess. That inspector's opinion of the remaining life expectancy of the heat pump caused the buyer to flee from the contract. Was he right? Who knows? As part of your exploratory meet and greet with the inspector, ask him how he will describe his findings during the inspection's post-summary meeting.

If you are representing the buyer, be sure you understand how the various inspectors like to work. Many home inspectors would prefer that you give them an hour or two to conduct their inspection and then meet with you and your buyer for a summary explanation of their findings. Following the inspector around like ducklings to their mother distracts the inspectors and may cause them to lose focus and miss something.

Some inspectors offer discounts to the buyer if they agree to pay for the inspection at the time of service. These discounts are offered as an incentive so the inspector doesn't have to wait for a closing that may never come. And why, you ask, might the closing not occur? Well, one reason may be because of the findings in the inspection report. But regardless of the reason, if the buyer decides to walk from the contract, the inspector may very well have to become an entirely different type of inspector (as in Inspector Clouseau) and chase the buyer all over town to receive payment for the services they provided on a house the buyer has no intention of buying. Talk with the inspector and if they offer this discount be sure to notify the buyer.

If you represent the seller, remember that the inspectors are hired by the buyer; they work for the buyer and they are usually paid for by the buyer. If you show up for the inspection and you ask for a recap, don't be surprised if the inspector blows you off. Years ago, acting as the listing agent, I showed up for an inspection in hopes of getting a head start on finding out what, if any, issues the home had. I was told by the inspector, using very colorful language, that I had no right to receive the information and no right to be there for the inspection. It is doubtful you will be allowed to participate in the inspection summary review with the buyer and buyer's agent and I doubt you should as you may cause an argument to ensue by trying to minimize an item the inspector pointed out. In general, you should wait for the buyer's agent to provide you a repair request list.

Repair request lists

I have represented the seller in several transactions in which the buyer's agent faxed over a copy of the inspection report summary pages asking the seller to repair every item on the list; as if this is an all-you-can-eat restaurant and the buyer is ordering everything from the menu. Does the buyer have the right to ask for every item, no matter how trivial, to be repaired by the seller? Of course they do. But I also think buyers and their agents need to think through their repair request lists instead of simply dumping it all on the seller's lap. Does the seller really need to replace the light bulb in the kitchen because the buyer has never owned a home before and *"couldn't possibly change that bulb!"* (Yes, that actually happened in one of my transactions and no we didn't close). Of course your fiduciary duties are to protect your client's interests and to put their needs above your own but that does not mean you should act as a puppet on a string passively reacting to whatever string your client happens to be pulling. Part of your fiduciary duties is to educate your client and help them understand the consequences and the reasonableness of their request for repairs. Of course the same holds true for listing agents when advising their sellers about making or refusing to make requested repairs.

One final note regarding repair lists; even though the inspection report belongs to the buyer and the seller has no right to review it without the buyer's permission, I think it is a very good idea to provide at least the pages of the report clearly describing the problem for which a repair has been requested. After all, if you are asking the seller to make a repair, why are you also asking them to play hide and seek in finding the issue by not providing the report to them? There are repair request forms and your firm may also provide its own form but please give consideration to also including the information and/or pictures from the inspector's report so the seller can clearly locate and address the item. I have heard agents say they don't like to do this because they don't want to give the seller a free inspection report. In my opinion, the list of requested repairs will give the seller a pretty good idea of the items that will show up again should they not make the repairs. I just believe that a copy of the inspector's findings fosters the making of those repairs by aiding the seller in knowing exactly what the inspector found and where the item in question is located. Let's work together and help each other complete the transaction by offering clear and concise communication regarding repair issues.

Working with lenders

There are mortgage brokers and lenders. They are not the same thing. A mortgage broker essentially does what you do... bring a buyer and a lender together. Mortgage brokers work with many different lenders and have many different loan packages available to buyers. A good mortgage broker is worth their weight in gold. They can make or break a deal, make the transaction go as smooth as skating on ice or as rough as riding a bucking bronco (probably the worst mixed metaphor I've used). It is critical and I mean *critical* that you get the buyer pre-approved before taxiing them around town to look at homes. Pre-approval means the mortgage broker has verified the information the buyer provided during the pre-qualification process. Our residential Offer to Purchase and Contract affords the buyer a negotiated Due Diligence Period in which the buyer must perform all of the activities they deem necessary to continue forward in the transaction. Assuring they can and will get a loan to buy the house is one of those items. You must speak with the mortgage broker or lender about the amount of time they need to process the loan to assure the buyer's loan is in final-approval during the Due Diligence Period. How long that takes varies from lender to lender. It is important to satisfy all of the lender's requirements during the Due Diligence Period. If the lender requests documentation the buyer cannot provide, or at least not provide to the satisfaction of the lender, and the contract is now outside of the Due Diligence Period, the buyer risks losing their Earnest Money and their Due Diligence Fee because of their inability to satisfy the lender's requirements thus resulting in their inability to close the transaction.

How silly can the lender's requests get? In one memorable transaction the buyer's best friend provided gift money and an accompanying gift letter clearly indicating that the gift money was not a loan and was not to be paid back. Normally gift moneys are only allowed from family but the bank made an exception in this case because the friend was a life-long friend. The bank only needed proof that they were life-long friends. And what might that proof be you ask? A photograph from when the two friends were children. How the bank knew this was, in fact, a childhood photograph of these two people and not two other children, I have no idea but they accepted it as proof and the loan was funded.

♠ Be sure to interview several mortgage brokers; their importance to the transaction cannot be overstated.

I believe you have every right to ask a buyer to be pre-approved before riding all over your local market trying to help them find the perfect home. In fact, in my opinion, not having them pre-approved is a breach of your fiduciary duties to your buyer client because without knowing exactly what amount of loan they are pre-approved for, you most likely will not know what homes to show them. Showing them homes in a price range that exceeds their budget is a breach of your fiduciary duties and the Realtor Code of Ethics.

"But the buyer said they can afford to spend $_____ ". Boy have I heard that one before. The only problem is the buyer doesn't realize that their low credit score is going to result in a higher interest rate or no loan at all. Please consult with your buyer about the importance of at least talking with a mortgage broker before viewing properties.

Working with appraisers

Although it is not a law, effective May 1, 2009 HVCC (Housing Valuation Code of Conduct) was agreed to between banks and our government in an attempt to ensure accurate appraisals and to shield appraisers from undue influence. It created a firewall that now prevents lenders and real estate agents from directly hiring appraisers. Its goal is to assure appraisers remain objective when performing appraisals and are not influenced by a lenders desire, or lack thereof, to fund a loan. The

218

effect of this agreement has had both positive and unintended negative effects on our industry. Although a discussion of these effects is beyond the scope of this book, I do want to point out that even though you are not allowed to hire the appraiser, you can talk to them and you can provide justification for the contracted sales price. Therefore, be sure you perform a Comparable Market Analysis (CMA) at the time of contract so, if necessary, you have justification for the agreed-to sales price.

Working with insurance companies

There is not much to say here because there are hundreds of choices; though I do want to point out a couple of things regarding your client's policies. Most, but not all, insurance companies consider the day of closing (i.e. your settlement meeting) as the day the buyer's policy goes into effect. What this means to you and your buyer is that even if the deed isn't recorded that day (proving ownership) the buyer's homeowner's policy is still in effect. Therefore, if the buyer causes damage and needs to file a claim (even though they don't yet own the house because the deed was not recorded) their insurance company will most likely pay the claim; but of course, I need to add the disclaimer that the buyer should always check with their insurance company before presuming this to be the case. In addition, the seller should keep their policy in place for several days after the settlement meeting and certainly until the deed is recorded. Insurance companies are required to prorate the seller's premium payment back to the day of settlement so it will not increase the seller's expenditures. The seller should do this, of course, as a just in case contingency plan. Finally, if your buyer wishes to execute a Buyer Possession before Closing agreement or the seller desires to carry out a Seller Possession after Closing agreement, be sure they talk with their respective insurance companies to assure they have proper coverage. Depending on the circumstances the buyer, or seller, would be considered a landlord and/or the buyer, or seller would be considered a tenant. In any case, these situations would not be covered under a standard homeowner's policy. I suppose I could have summarized this discussion by simply saying, *"Be sure your clients check with their homeowner insurance company in all transactions..."* but what fun would that have been?

Working with closing attorneys

As with all service providers, hiring the right attorney is important. Typically the buyer hires the attorney, but they will lean heavily on your advice in choosing an attorney; particularly if they are from out of town. Again, talk with agents and your BIC about the attorneys they use. The one piece of advice I can offer is to be sure you determine whether that attorney is willing to offer their advice and counsel should an issue arise, or are they going to defer to the buyer and seller. The buyer hires the attorney and the attorney should protect the buyer's interests but I have been to closings where an issue has arisen and the attorney offered no opinion or advice. In one closing I had to say to the attorney, *"the buyer hired you, please answer their question."* (Ok, I admit, I don't think I was that nice about it.) Be sure you thoroughly investigate recommended closing attorneys. Also note that the paralegal is, dare I say, more important than the attorney because they coordinate the closing and handle all the paperwork.

I have never received a referral from my favorite attorney and I don't expect to since she works with many real estate agents and it would be political and business suicide to favor one agent over another. But what I do get from her is a quick and accurate response to any question I've ever asked. That to me is worth more than any referral she might throw my way.

A final note on service providers

Be sure to keep a list of service providers handy. Contact each of them and introduce yourself. Let them know you're new to the business and you would like to either have a cup of coffee with them or take five minutes of their time to introduce yourself. Having a face with a name is important; especially if you need a quick answer in an emergency situation.

Finally Appendix E contains a list of service provider categories you should consider researching, with blank lines so you can fill in each provider's contact information.

Trail Log:

_____

_____

_____

_____

_____

_____

_____

_____

_____

_____

_____

_____

_____

_____

_____

_____

_____

_____

_____

_____

_____

_____

_____

_____

_____

_____

_____

_____

_____

_____

_____

Chapter 20: Trail hygiene, culture and proper etiquette.

Trail culture and etiquette or how to behave properly

The 80/20 rule is alive and well. 80% of the business is done by 20% of the businesses. In real estate I would argue that the rule is more like 90/10. 90% of the business is done by 10% of the agents. The trick, of course, is to be in that 10% club. Work the system, be diligent, be consistent and you too can be an exclusive member of this club (jackets optional).

With this pattern of activity, the odds are you will frequently interact with the same agents. Be mindful of this and treat other agents with great respect and professionalism. The odds are pretty good that you will run into them again.

Here is an excellent piece of advice I heard a BIC say to one of her agents, *"It's your commission, go get it."* At first I thought she was scolding the agent but in retrospect I now believe she was telling him that even if the problem was not his fault, he should help the other agent solve it so they could close the transaction and get paid. Good advice. I suppose another way to say this is, just because it's not your fault, doesn't mean it's not your problem.

Remember, you will run across all skill levels in this business. Some agents will be newer than you and know less than you. Some agents will have been in the business for years, but are still doing business as if times haven't changed at all. Be forgiving. Be generous with your time, talents, and knowledge. Help other agents become successful and you will too.

The real estate industry still ranks poorly in customer service satisfaction surveys. There is only one way to improve our scores and the perception of our industry and that is for all of us to chip in and lift each other up. Hikers on the AT don't walk by another hiker sitting on the side of the trail, they ask if they are ok, if they need help, and if they do help is offered. Be the kind of agent that offers help when it is needed. If you can help resolve the issue without violating your fiduciary duties to your client, do so.

Dress for success

I know this may sound silly but there is such a thing as dress for success. Would you rather do business with someone who just rolled out of bed, unwashed and unkempt or with someone who is dressed, ready to go and bright eyed and bushy tailed? I know it shouldn't be this way. We should be judged solely on our abilities, our knowledge, and our skills and not on how we look. I would agree with you if we were sitting in a windowless room writing code for Microsoft but we're not. We're out there in the real world and impressions matter. Argue with me all you want but I didn't make the rule, I'm just hoping you'll understand the rule and whether you agree with it or not, you'll abide by it by dressing appropriately.

Unfortunately, I have to say the younger you are, the more important it is to dress professionally because many of your potential clients will be the same age as your parents. You will need to not only impress them with your real estate knowledge but your seriousness toward your career. The sloppier you look, the more you will have to impress them with your knowledge and as a new agent is that a fair expectation of yourself?

If it makes you feel better, regardless of your age you need only dress one level above your prospective client. If you market to the Lake Norman area in Mecklenburg County or Asheville or the beach area, khaki pants and a professional looking shirt (i.e. no T-shirts) would probably suffice. However there are other markets that require at least a sport jacket, if not a suit and tie.

You can dress how you want but I'm just warning you, you may never know that the reason you didn't get that sweet $400,000 listing was because the retired husband, having spent 35 years as a mid-level manager at Bank of America, felt you couldn't be a serious agent based on the way you dressed for the meeting. Do you want to say you did it your way or do you want the listing?

With that said, I would like your permission to talk about sex appeal for a moment. If you would prefer not to read what I have to say, please accept my apologies and skip to the section titled First Impressions. If you're still here, indulge me for a moment... They say that sex sells and I suppose for many products it does. But let me ask you something, if the product is truly everything they say it is would it really need the scantily clad woman or the buff man to help sell it? I personally believe that eventually the product would stand on its own merits. In other words, sex may sell but ultimately the product has to be made well and do what it says it will do or it will eventually fail. You are the product. I would ask that you consider standing on the merits of your market knowledge, computer skills, negotiating prowess, marketing channel acumen, and people skills. I have seen my fair share of agents – men and women (and I'm sure you have too) who try to put their best assets forward, if you catch my drift. From skimpy dresses, tight jeans, stiletto heels, glamour shots, the list goes on and on.

I am not a prude; in fact, I'm far from it but I do believe there is a time and place for everything. Have you ever had a cup of coffee with a friend at a local coffee house and commented on how someone was dressed? Of course you have because we all have... guess what they're doing the same with you.

I am certainly not suggesting you dress like an old schoolmarm or stereotypical librarian, but I do think it is reasonable, professional, and more than likely to help you grow your business if you dress so the other gender's eyes are looking at your eyes and not, how shall I say this, other areas of your body.

A quick closing thought and then I'm off my rant... if you interview for a listing and you are dressed in a way that causes one of the spouses to study you in an inappropriate way, you may have inadvertently created that evening's argument once you leave; and a strong chance you won't get that listing. Of course after reading this brief diatribe, you may now be thinking, *"They don't have to look!"* and I suppose that's true but if it is true then why dress that way at all?

First impressions

In my opinion, if you plan to be in public, why wouldn't you always want to look your best and wear your name tag? Think of it this way, if you had a store wouldn't you have a sign out front? You are your store and your store is as mobile as you are and instead of customers coming to you, you go to them. In our business first impressions do matter; so dress the part, wear your name tag and smile. Recognize that when you are out doing errands, there is always an opportunity to meet someone interested in buying or selling or at least wanting to talk about real estate.

By the way, if you decide to place a magnetic sign on your car, consider it the equivalent of the *"how's my driving"* bumper sticker you see on commercial vehicles. Oh and I'm sure this goes without saying, be careful about how you "wave" to other drivers.

Trail Log:

Chapter 21: Trail safety.

Safety is of utmost importance. This can be a lonely business and you can spend long stretches of time with buyers and sellers you have just met or know little about. **The NC RE Commission publishes a Safety Brochure, read it!**

In general I personally think agents could do a better job with safety. I have been guilty of running off to meet a buyer I've never met and you will too. I suppose it is human nature to trust our fellow man and woman. But you need to learn to ignore that inborn belief and learn to follow safety protocol – whether your own and, should they have one, your firm's policy.

The "12 second rule"

Disclaimer: The 12 second rule is meant to act as a guideline in the absence of a policy with your office. Please read, review and abide by your office's policy.

- Take 2 seconds when you arrive at a home
    - Is there questionable activity?
    - Are you parked in a well-lit area?
    - Can you be blocked in?

- Take 2 seconds after you step out of the car
    - Are there suspicious-looking people around?
    - Do you know where you are going?
    - What is the buyer wearing? Is it loose/baggy clothes with lots of pockets? Could their intentions be to leave with more than they came with?
- Take 2 seconds as you walk toward your destination
    - Do you see any obstacles or hiding places in the area?
    - Is anyone loitering in the area?

- Take 2 seconds at the door
    - Do you have an uneasy feeling?
    - Are you letting the buyer lead or at least be at your side? There is never a reason the buyer needs to be behind you

as you walk through the home.

- Take 2 seconds as soon as you enter
  - LISTEN FIRST for out of place noises.
  - Does anything seem out of place?
  - Is anyone present who shouldn't be there.

- Take 2 seconds as you walk through
  - Are doors closed? (knock firmly)
  - Is there a basement? Be sure to check for the light switch.
  - Are there darkened areas or other areas that could trap you?

The rule of "always"
- Always meet prospects at the office or another public place.
  - Make copies or write down identification information.
- Always tell someone where you're going.
- Always have ICE (In Case of Emergency) loaded in your phone's address book.
- Always have a coded message in case you're in trouble.
- **Always listen to your gut feel.**
- Always remember, "It is better to ask forgiveness than permission."
- Always have a charged cell phone or a charger backup.
- Always wear shoes you could run in should you need to. I've never worn stiletto heels but I would guess they are a bit difficult to run in.

The rule of "never"
- Never become lazy or lax.
- Never assume it can't happen to you.
- Never assume that just because you have met the prospect or know them that you are always safe!
- Never hesitate to call 9-1-1.

- Never use glamour shots!
- Never wear inordinate amounts of jewelry.
- Never carry large amounts of cash.

I may be a little over the top with some of these suggestions. Sadly though I have personally known and heard of agents being robbed, raped, killed or harmed in other ways. I won't apologize for being concerned for your safety and neither should you.

The show "Hill Street Blues" said it best... *"Let's be careful out there!"*

Trail Log:

_____
_____
_____
_____
_____
_____
_____
_____
_____
_____
_____
_____
_____
_____
_____
_____
_____
_____
_____
_____
_____

At trail's end

What an adventure, this real estate hike. What views, and what wondrous animals you'll meet along the way. Real estate is not the easiest path to choose in life. Many have failed on its sometimes treacherous trails. Consistency is the key to success in this business. Always push yourself. Set goals and strive to accomplish them. If you fall short of a goal, reset and try again. Learn from your mistakes. Remember that at the end of the day you are your own boss. You set the agenda, you set your schedule and you set your goals. You decide what you will and won't earn based on your efforts. Sure, you will have help along the way, especially if you ask for it, but in the end, it will be you putting one foot in front of the other until you have arrived at your destination. Keep up with the latest technologies but be sure you purchase only the gear best suited to help you achieve your goals. Watch your marketing dollars to be sure you are, at a minimum, breaking even and be sure you always ask how someone found out about you so you can record what is working and what isn't. Discover your ideal path with your BIG WHY and your elevator speech. If you are having a bad day, give yourself a break. Rest and recuperate, take a walk or work out; do what it takes to help you get back in the game. Practice your scripts, your closing techniques, and your presentations. Study your contracts and get to know the housing inventory. And finally, remember that no one requires you to be successful, it is optional, but so too is failing... Which option will you choose?

If you are willing to do what 82% of other real estate agents are not willing to do, you will be successful. Walk this trail with me and do not be afraid to succeed.

Appendix A: The BIG WHY exercise

Of all the questions we can ask, the most revealing is "Why?" Like
layers of an onion every time this question is asked another layer of truth
is peeled away. Psychologists say we need to ask why five times to get to
the truth of something. It would be easy then to list the word why five
times and ask you to answer that question each time until we uncover
your BIG WHY... it would be easy but unless I was sitting across from
you helping you interpret and build on your answers it would not be
terribly effective so let's try another strategy to uncover your BIG WHY.
In working this exercise, go as quickly as you can and don't rule
anything out; simply put your thoughts down based on the question
asked...

1) There are thousands of opportunities and career paths, why real
   estate?

_____

_____

_____

_____

_____

_____

_____

_____

_____

2) What do you hope to accomplish with your real estate career?

_____

_____

_____

_____

_____

_____

_____

3) What are the reasons you want to accomplish these things?

_____
_____
_____
_____
_____
_____

4) Of these reasons, what one is the most important to you?

_____
_____
_____
_____

5) Why is it more important than the other reasons given?

_____
_____
_____
_____
_____

6) What would happen if you were not able to accomplish or fulfill this reason?

_____
_____
_____
_____
_____

7) Is there another field of work that could also fulfill this reason? If so, what is it and why aren't you choosing that career path?

_____

_____

_____

_____

_____

_____

8) Will you know when you have fulfilled this reason? (Yes or No) What will that look like?

_____

_____

_____

_____

_____

9) How will you feel and what reward will you give yourself when you have fulfilled this reason?

_____

_____

_____

_____

_____

_____

The answers to these questions will help you paint your BIG WHY picture. Share your findings with those close to you, so they can help you stay on track. Always keep this picture in mind, particularly when times are tough, it is the driving force behind your business.

Appendix B: Your first week checklist

Disclosure: Until you affiliate yourself with a firm and you are under the supervision of a BIC, you may not hold yourself as being available to help others buy, sell or lease real estate. Do not make the mistake of running around telling your friends that you have your license and you're ready to help them. You'll be ready when you affiliate with a firm. Please make sure you follow this all important NC Real Estate Commission rule. *"Can I at least tell them I got my license?"* you ask. Sure, just be sure they understand you cannot hold yourself out as an active agent available to assist them in any given real estate transaction.

I am not going to discuss your first week once you've chosen a firm because I assume that when you interviewed them, you made sure they had a plan of action for you and they will guide you through your first week. This list is designed for your first week after you received your license, but before you've joined a firm, so you can get a jump start on your business. These are items you will want to check off no matter what firm you join.

Your first week's checklist:

- ☐ Using either a spreadsheet program, a database program, Microsoft word, index cards or pen and paper, create a list of names, numbers, email addresses, phone numbers and addresses of everyone you know or know of. Use multiple resources to compile your list:
  - o Church directory
  - o School directory
  - o Check book register
  - o Past meetings on your calendar
  - o Neighbors
  - o Your children's and spouse's/significant other's friends and families
  - o Contractors and other providers of service
  - o Co-workers from current and former jobs

- o Facebook and/or LinkedIn contacts
- o Family members including your extended family (all the way to that 3rd cousin twice removed on your mother's great aunt's uncle's side)
- o Local businesses you frequent
- o Don't dismiss people you know but don't particularly like
- o Other _____
- o Other _____
- o Other _____
- o Other _____

Now I don't want you to panic here. I'm not asking you to contact all of these people, just compile the list. We are merely brain storming and building a contact database. Your goal is to compile as many names as you can. You'll be surprised how many people you know; especially if you don't limit yourself. Consider playing the Kevin Bacon game *six degrees of separation* to really expand your list.

Once you have compiled this list, assign letter grades to each contact. In other words, you are to define your inner-circle, your mid-circle, and your outer-circle of contacts. An "A" would indicate an inner-circle candidate, one you would contact early and often. Your A list contains people you could call and say to them *"I need buyers, find me a buyer!"* and they wouldn't be offended; in fact they would take your request to heart. Your "B" group is people you are very familiar with but you may not feel comfortable making the above statement. Your "C" contains people that know you. Your objective with the C list is to either move them into the A and B group or drop them.

- ☐ If you are a Provisional Broker, schedule your first post-licensing class.
- ☐ Place on your calendar a repeating meeting notice to schedule your required CE early in the CE season.
- ☐ Begin developing your 10 second elevator speech.
- ☐ Set up interviews with several firms (not necessarily to be scheduled in your first week, just get the meetings set up.)

☐ Start studying and practice explaining the following forms:
  o Working with Real Estate Agents Brochure.
  o Exclusive Right to Sell Listing Agreement (if you can't get one, review the one in your Pre-License book).
  o Offer to Purchase and Contract (Pre-License book).
  o Exclusive Buyer Agency Agreement Form (Pre-License book).
  o Addenda associated with residential sales (Pre-License book).

☐ Begin reading everything you can about the local, regional and national real estate markets.
  o Review inman.com (a real estate and real estate technology website)
  o The public pages of Realtor.com
  o RealtyTimes.com (a market conditions report by county and written by local agents. Want to see what your future competition thinks? Check this site out)
  o Review the various firms' websites and Facebook pages you have an interest in joining.

Subsequent weeks' activities
Even if you have not chosen a firm within the first few weeks, there are still activities you need to work on.
  o Start looking at neighborhoods you may be interested in farming (see "farming" below). Study them on Realtor.com, Zillow.com and/or Trulia.com. Review the tax records and Google the neighborhood. In other words, learn everything you can about that neighborhood so you can hit the ground running when you join a firm.

  o **Farming** a neighborhood means you canvas it with flyers, door knocks, ice-cream socials, etc… whatever it takes to become the dominant agent in that neighborhood. It is a medium to long term strategy but it can be an excellent way to develop your business should you get yourself established. Think of neighborhoods you're familiar with. Who is the dominant agent in

235

there? If it can work for them it can work for you. You may be thinking that the neighborhood you want to farm is already dominated by an agent so how can you possibly get a toe-hold? Well they may be the dominant agent now, but just like the game "king (or queen) of the mountain" they weren't always on top.

↑ Some firms have a policy on multiple agents farming the same neighborhood so if you have one in mind, see if that firm will allow you to farm it.

☐ If you are now with a firm
  o Create a signature for your emails so people know your firm, your phone, your website, your picture and icons linking to at least these websites:
    ▪ Facebook (set up a personal and business profile if necessary)
    ▪ Twitter
    ▪ LinkedIn
    ▪ Blog site (if applicable)
    ▪ And of course your website.
    ▪ Other sites that you want an email recipient to be able to click to.

  o Set up your profile at:
    ▪ Zillow.com
    ▪ Trulia.com
    ▪ Homes.com
    ▪ Realtor.com

☐ Your list of activities

_____

_____

_____

Appendix C: Your education requirements and fee reminders

☐ Complete post licensing:
- 301 Broker Relations
- 302 Contracts to Closing
- 303 Miscellaneous Topics

- Note the courses can be taken in any order and all may be done in your first year, but you must successfully complete at least one per year from the date you received your license or your license will be set to inactive status, which can also be read to say, *"You're out of business!"*
- Each course has an in-class exam that you must pass.
- Post licensing does not count toward your Continuing Education (see Continuing Education below).
- One other note regarding Post-licensing. Should you decide to pursue your GRI (a 90 hour three tiered course) the GRI designation replaces the 303 Miscellaneous Topics course. Of course this means more time in the classroom but you also get the GRI designation. (Read my thoughts on furthering your education "Becoming a trail master" in chapter two.)

☐ Continuing Education (CE):
- Each year all real estate agents must successfully complete eight hours of continuing education.
- Four hours is the Mandatory Update that ALL real estate agents must take.
- Four hours is an elective that may be completed in the classroom or online.
- CE must be completed between July first of the current calendar year and June tenth of the next calendar year.
- The real estate commission does not require you to take CE in the first year you received your license (75 hours is enough don't you think?). However, starting with the upcoming July first, you must complete your eight hours by the next June tenth.

☐ Annual fee:

    – The NC Real Estate Commission requires all real estate licensees to pay an annual renewal fee by June 30th of every year. Do not be late or you will also pay a penalty.

    – The National Association of Realtors requires dues to be paid at year end.

    – Your local MLS also has dues monthly, semi-annually or quarterly.

    – North Carolina's Secretary of State also charges a privilege license fee for the privilege of doing business in North Carolina.

    – There may be other fees. Check with your real estate firm's BIC.

    – **Put these fees on your calendar so you don't forget to pay them.**

Appendix D: Suggested questions you should ask real estate firms during the interview

I planned to write a detailed list of questions you should ask prospective firms but occasionally we are blessed to have people in our life that know a whole lot more than we do. I am one of the lucky ones to have such a person. Len Elder is an attorney, national trainer, Realtor, motivational speaker and one of the smartest people I have ever met. He owns and operates a national company called "Course Creators"; check them out at www.coursecreators.com. They specialize in helping Realtors gain a technological edge in this ever-changing real estate world. If you ever have a chance to attend one of Len's classes, **do it.** It is an investment you will see an immediate return on.

I give you Len Elder's exceptional list of questions you should ask firms during your interview process…

WHAT ARE THE RIGHT QUESTIONS TO ASK YOUR BROKER BEFORE YOU AGREE TO WORK FOR THEM?

By Len Elder, DREI

There are lots of lists that people have prepared of questions to ask any brokerage firm before you go to work with them. Below are over 100 questions that you may want to ask and Realty Times has their own list of questions available to licensees shopping brokerage firms at the following link:

http://www.realtytimes.com/rtpages/20040130_questions.htm.

I think the decision is incredibly personal and that the questions that are asked ought to help the agent determine whether or not they and the brokerage are a "good fit." In other words, how well does what you need and expect from a brokerage pair up with what the brokerage has to offer. I would suggest that before you go by anyone else's list that you ought to create your own based on your particular desires, needs and ambitions. For me personally I can narrow the list greatly. There are only 10 questions I would ask, I have indicated the reasons I would ask them because I think the reason is more important than the question.

1. **What is the Company's mission statement and value beliefs?**
   I want to know if the company and I have compatible beliefs and mission statements. Does the company put the same priority on things that I do?

2. **What type of training and educational opportunities does the brokerage support?**
   Today, education and training are more important than ever. I want to know what the brokerage is doing to train and educate its agents and what type of resources are available.

Describe the working environment for me?

   I want to know whether the work environment is suitable for the way in which I know I work best. Some people want a quiet place of solitude to work. By the way, that is not me, I am looking for a collaborative interactive environment and I want to know if that is valued or encouraged.

3. **Why do you want to hire me?**
   I want to know that I more than a number and that there is a particular reason that the brokerage thinks that I can benefit them other than just being another statistic in the pool of licensed agents.

4. **What kind of help and support will I receive with my business plan?**
   Being successful in real estate is being successful at running your own business; I want to know what kind of support I will get in planning and growing my career.

5. **What type of resources does the brokerage provide?**

I want to know that the brokerage provides resources and benefits that will help me grow and that my association with a particular firm gives me some additional leverage.

6. **What are the names of some current agents I can talk to?**
   I realize I am more likely to get the straight story from agents who currently work for the firm. I want to be able to see if I can relate with these people and whether they are the type of people I will be able to associate with.

7. **Who will I be directly working with?**
   Most firms operate with various offices and not all offices are equal. I want to know specifically who will be my mentor, leader or support system and feel that I can work comfortably with that individual regardless of how I feel about the firm.

8. **Can I talk to my potential immediate supervisor?**
   A personal meeting with the individual with whom I will be working most closely will allow me to determine whether the two of us are "a fit".

9. **What do you see as the future of real estate?**
   Real estate is constantly changing and evolving. I want to know that the brokerage has at least given some thought to the future and I am able to rely on the fact that they will help guide me in the right direction.

100 Questions to ask any brokerage
Company Background & Presence

1. Can you give me a brief history of the Company? Who are the owners? Why was it started?
2. Is the company an independent operation or a franchise?
3. How many offices do they have and where are they?
4. History of the current management?
5. Does the company have a mission statement? Values? Core beliefs?

6. How many agents work here? How many are new agents? Experienced?
7. How many agents would bring you to capacity?
8. What is your typical turnover rate of agents?
9. What professional designations do your agents hold?
10. What is the historical record of closed volume this office has done?
11. What type of market penetration numbers do you have?
12. What affiliations does the company have?
13. Does the company own affiliated businesses? Do the agents share in this?

Real Estate Training Programs

1. Tell me about your training philosophy?
2. Do you have a New Agent training program? How is it structured?
3. Can I see the program?
4. What is the cost of the program?
5. Who are the instructors and what are their backgrounds?
6. Where is it held and at what times?
7. Is fieldwork encouraged during the program?
8. Is there a follow-up career launch type program to help get started?
9. Is there a system in place to encourage early accountability?
10. What Board of Realtors training is available?
11. What type of ongoing training do you do? Can I see your training calendar?
12. Is there an office orientation program?
13. What type of advanced training is available and who teaches it?
14. Do any courses provide licensing credit?

Building Your Real Estate Business

1. Does the company have a philosophy on how I should build my business?
2. How does the company help me establish priorities and goals? Examples?

3. Do we receive help establishing a business plan?
4. Can I "brand" myself and my business? If so, how?
5. What legal status do I assume with the company? Independent Contractor or otherwise?
6. Is there a contract required? Can I see a copy?
7. Do you have a Policy/Procedures Manual? May I see it? Do I receive my own copy?
8. Does the company offer systems to help build my business? What are they?
9. In regard to building my branding:
10. What does your signage look like? Are there options?
11. Are personal logos (slogans) allowed?
12. What card design is used? Flexibility?
13. Collateral and advertising materials you use?
14. Can I acquire Builder accounts on my own? If not, how are they handled and at what cost?
15. Can I acquire Relocation accounts on my own? If not, how are they handled and at what cost?
16. How does the company handle incoming referrals? Do your agents consider this a fair system?
17. Does the company have an advertising policy? Explain how it works? Who pays for it? Can I do my own advertising?
18. How are sign and ad calls handled in the company?
19. Do you have a floor time requirement?
20. Can I direct my own sign and advertisement calls to me directly?
21. Do you require Errors & Omissions insurance? Who pays for it? What happens if there is an overage in that account collected from the agents?
22. What is my exposure in the event of a lawsuit?
23. Do you help with my accounting?
24. If our relationship is not successful, who owns the rights to my listings?
25. If I were to leave, how are my pending commissions handled?

Economic Programs
1. How does your commission/compensation program work?
2. Can you take me through a "live" example by the numbers?

3. What is the office procedure for getting paid on a closing?
4. Are agents in the office on different plans? Explain them?
5. What is the initial and ongoing cost of my affiliation with the company?
6. Can I hire a personal assistant? Can they be licensed? Does the company charge me a fee for the assistant? What commission program does the assistant fall under?
7. Do you have a profit sharing program with agents? How does it work?
8. Are there other investment opportunities within the company? How do they work?
9. What is the policy and cost if I buy or sell real estate personally?

Real Estate Office Management
1. What are the manager's priorities and basic responsibilities?
2. Do they list or sell property as agents of the firm?
3. Describe the additional staff and their responsibilities?
4. Is agent input encouraged? If so, how is it acquired?
5. Describe your meetings in the office? The frequency? Is attendance required?
6. Who establishes Office Policies?
7. Describe the type of culture you create in the office? How is this done?
8. List the reasons an agent would be asked to leave your firm and why?
9. Do you share the company books with the agents? If so, how often?
10. How are "housekeeping" items conveyed to the agents?

Real Estate Technology
1. What is the company's basic philosophy in regard to using technology?
2. Does the company provide high-speed internet access and at what cost?
3. Are the printers/computers/machines in the office networked? Can I hook into this network?
4. Do you provide specific software/ what are the programs?

5. Do you provide voicemail?
6. Do you provide e-mail? Is it private?
7. Do you provide a web site for the agents?
8. Do you provide any type of computer training?
9. Do you provide software training?
10. Does the company have a web site? An Intranet site?
11. Are their presentations available that are electronic from the company?
12. Do you encourage using Personal Data (palm pilots) Assistants? How?
13. Does the company provide marketing templates?
14. Does the company provide forecasting electronically?
15. Can I do my accounting electronically?
16. What type of long-term technology support can the company offer?

Office Environment

1. Does the office look like a professional environment?
2. Who and how are customers and clients greeted?
3. How many conference rooms are there?
4. How many research rooms are there? Can you look at them?
5. How many computers for general use and what software do they have?
6. Printer situation? High speed/Color/Laser?
7. How are incoming and outgoing faxes handled?
8. Copier situation? Cost associated with them?
9. Other research tools available to help you? What are they?
10. Do they maintain a training facility? Can you see it?
11. Do they maintain a computer lab?
12. Is the general office cramped?
13. Is there adequate parking? For agents and customer / clients?
14. What type of desk arrangements are there? What are the specific policies on this?

Here are a few of my own.

- Before even visiting the firm, Google them. Are there public criticisms of the company? How about people singing their praises? Do they have a Facebook presence and if so what are people saying about them?

- Are you allowed to talk to more than just one agent or will they steer you to their "favorite son"?

- Have the agents share with you two or three challenges they faced in growing their business. How has the company helped them overcome those challenges?

- How available is the BIC to answer questions or should you talk with the administrative staff? (If they indicate that the administrative staff is your best source. That may be a red flag that the BIC will not be available when you need them most.)

- Are you willing to role play with me should I need or want it?

- Are you a competing BIC? If so, how do you handle situations where you and a Provisional Broker are in the same transaction? (They better have an answer because a Provisional Broker and the BIC cannot be designated agents in the same transaction.)

- What are your desk fees, copy fees, and what other fees might I be expected to pay?

- What is your brokerage split? Do you offer bonuses for internal sales? Do you require your agents to emphasize the firm's listings over other companies' listings? (If they do this may be a "red flag" of how they carry out and understand their fiduciary duties.)

- Will I have my own website or a page on the firm's website?

Your questions:

_____
_____
_____
_____
_____
_____
_____
_____
_____
_____
_____
_____
_____
_____
_____
_____
_____
_____
_____
_____
_____
_____
_____
_____
_____
_____
_____
_____
_____
_____
_____

Appendix E: Vendor list and suggested resources

Disclosure: Although I cannot recommend specific companies, I can provide categories of businesses you need to start cultivating. If you aren't aware of specific companies discuss this with your BIC or other agents in your office. You will want to get at least two companies in each category on your "team". Don't expect them to provide you with referrals because they are on other agent's teams too but they should be available to answer questions when needed and they should provide excellent service to your clients.

☐ Closing attorney
   - _____
   - _____
   - _____

☐ Mechanical/Structural Inspector
   - _____
   - _____
   - _____

☐ Termite/Wood Destroying Insect Inspector
   - _____
   - _____
   - _____

☐ Appraiser
   - _____
   - _____
   - _____

☐ Lender/Mortgage Broker
   - _____
   - _____
   - _____

- [ ] Radon Inspector
  - o _____
  - o _____
  - o _____

- [ ] EFIS (Synthetic Stucco) Siding Inspector
  - o _____
  - o _____
  - o _____

- [ ] Sign maker/marketing company (if your firm doesn't provide)
  - o _____
  - o _____
  - o _____

- [ ] Home Owner Warranty Company
  - o _____
  - o _____
  - o _____

- [ ] Home Owner Insurance Company
  - o _____
  - o _____
  - o _____

- [ ] Well/Septic Inspection Company
  - o _____
  - o _____
  - o _____

- [ ] Pool Inspector
  - o _____
  - o _____
  - o _____

☐ Under Ground Storage Tank Inspector

    ○ _____

    ○ _____

    ○ _____

Providers specific to your market

Category: _____

    ○ _____

    ○ _____

    ○ _____

Category: _____

    ○ _____

    ○ _____

    ○ _____

Category: _____

    ○ _____

    ○ _____

    ○ _____

Category: _____

    ○ _____

    ○ _____

    ○ _____

Category: _____

    ○ _____

    ○ _____

    ○ _____

Useful resources

There are many websites available to you to assist you in your business. In writing this book I was going to list those sites but with the speed the internet changes, those sites may not exist by the time you read this book; so I am providing the site's domain name but also the definitions that you should Google to find out more.

- QR Codes: QR stands for Quick Response. It is essentially a bar code smart phones can scan and then display the results of that scan (you must download an App to read them). What can we use them for? You can place a QR code on the back of your business card and when scanned the smart phone can display your uploaded YouTube video. Or you can create a QR code to direct the user to your website or send you a text message. If you can imagine it, QR codes can probably be used to advertise it. To view a functional QR codes, see the end of this appendix. http://qrcode.kaywa.com/

- Drip email campaigns. How would you like to be able to go about your work while your computer automatically sends out regular emails to keep your past clients, friends and family aware of your real estate business? This is the essence of drip email campaigns. Many real estate firms now offer this but there are a few websites that also provide this service. www.happygrasshopper.com contacts the first 50 email addresses you upload, for free.

- Online document storage and retrieval. If you are like most people, you rarely, if ever back up your computer's hard-drive; big mistake, but typical. By using online storage you never have to worry about losing your data and you can retrieve it from anywhere that has internet access. www.dropbox.com provides up to 500 MB free online storage and retrieval and for most people 500 MB is more than enough storage space; particularly if all you're storing is documents. If, however, you require more space you can purchase it at a very low rate.

Also check out SkyDrive from Microsoft. It works like Dropbox but they offer more space for free.

🖳 Top real estate sites
  o Zillow.com
  o Trulia.com
  o Realtor.com
  o Homes.com
  o Realestateabc.com

🖳 www.youtube.com. It is a very good bet this site will be around for awhile. I placed it under useful resources because although we have seen that it can be an enormous waste of time, it also provides an almost unlimited number of helpful videos. If you're not sure how to do something, search Youtube. It is a very good bet that there will be a helpful video. Further, as I mentioned earlier in the book, you can create your own "Channel" and upload your video tours. There are several how to videos that teach you how to create your own channel (guess which site has them) so I won't go into detail here.

🖳 www.google.com Of all the sites mentioned and available resources Google is your one-stop-shop. It is the most popular and largest search engine on the web.

Keeping up with technology

In summary, keeping up with technology can be very intimidating and, potentially, time consuming. Instead of trying to keep up with all the latest and greatest technologies, follow this strategy to keep up with only those areas you need.

- Assess your needs. Make sure the products fit your needs and not the other way around. What are you doing that technology can do cheaper and/or easier?

252

- Research (by this I mean Google or visit the library) the resources available to assist you.

- Rank these resources based on:
  - Ease of use.
  - Extraneous/unnecessary features that may add to the cost or learning curve.
  - Cost (a more expensive item may be easier to use, saving you time and money in the long run).
  - Product support help line and/or a try it before you buy it option?
  - Dedicate a few hours a day getting to know the product and make your decision during the try it before you buy it window.

- Subscribe to a national magazine or Ezine (online magazine). Most, if not all, will discuss the major trends of technology and the direction technology is going. You do not need to be a "techie" spending hours reading every article; use these subscriptions to get a general overview and as you see a product that helps you solve a need, research that product further.

Of course it goes without saying (but I'll say it anyway) that you must read the National Association of Realtor magazine and your state and regional Realtor magazines. Why so many of us chose not read them is unfathomable.

Visit us at www.WilsonRealtync.com   Find us on

Appendix F: Checklists

- How do I Plan for This Move? A Guide for Sellers and buyers
- Top 10 Maintenance Items you can Address for Little to No Cost
- Seller Listing Paperwork Checklist
- Exclusive Right to Represent Buyer Checklist
- Buyer/Seller OTP&C Paperwork Checklist

A moving guide for buyers and sellers

8 Weeks before your move date...

- ❑ If applicable, contact a professional mover or truck rental company and get estimates: Make early reservations.
- ❑ Decide what furniture stays and what furniture goes.
- ❑ If you rented a temporary storage unit, contact them to finalize your bill.
- ❑ Make plans to hold a garage sale.
- ❑ Use up or plan to recycle the things that can't or won't be moved (for cans of paint, open the lids so the paint can dry before being discarded), aerosol cleaning supplies, perishable/frozen food.
- ❑ Call the Visitor Center or Chamber of Commerce to receive information about your new community.
- ❑ If applicable, make travel and hotel arrangements.
- ❑ Take pictures to remember your old home, if desired.

6 weeks before your move date...

- ❑ Inventory your possessions and determine what will be sold or donated.
- ❑ Record serial numbers of items you're moving
- ❑ Consider video-taping all items to be put on the truck to record their condition.
- ❑ Get copies of records from your dentist, doctor, attorney, CPA, etc. Transfer your children's school records. And get recommendations for new service providers.
- ❑ Contact investment managers and banks for change of address.
- ❑ Establish bank accounts at new address.
- ❑ Transfer bank accounts and cancel any direct deposit or Automatic Payment plans, if applicable.
- ❑ Get a change of address kit from the Post Office and start sending the cards out.
- ❑ Email your change of address to friends, family and business acquaintances.

4 weeks before your move date...

❑ Host a garage sale. Recycle, donate or discard those things that don't sell.

❑ Repair holes in the walls and other minor blemishes.

3 weeks before your move date...

❑ Assemble packing materials: dolly, scissors, packing tape, bubble wrap, newspaper, string, boxes, etc...

❑ Begin packing items you don't need.

❑ Arrange to cancel utilities at your current house and establish them at your new home. The Visitor Center information packet should contain providers of service).

❑ Get car license, registration and insurance in order.

2 weeks before the move date...

❑ Make special arrangements for moving pets. Consult with veterinarian for tips on making moving easier on your pet.

❑ Get your car(s) checked and serviced for the trip.

❑ Transfer all medical prescriptions to the pharmacy in your new location.

❑ Return library books and DVDs.

❑ Send out dry-cleaning.

❑ Pick up any tools or other items that were loaned to friends, family or neighbors.

1 week before the move date...

❑ Pick up all dry cleaning.

❑ Finish major packing, label boxes by content, floor and room destination.

❑ If using movers, contact them to be sure there's been no scheduling errors.

2 or 3 days before the move date...

❑ Defrost and clean the refrigerator.

❑ Stop by your bank and pick up extra cash or traveler checks.

❑ Pack a "weekend bag" in case of delay.

❏ Pack a "Move-In Handy Items" box that contains: scissors, utility knife, and preparation for coffee making, radio, soap, camera, paper and pen, toiletries (including toilet paper). Pack this in your car last to be accessed first.

Moving day...
❏ If applicable, pick up the rental truck early.
❏ Inspect basement, attic, crawl space and other oft forgotten storage places.
❏ If there is a delay between your move out and the new owner's move in: Turn off main water valve, turn off electricity at breaker box, disconnect garage door from automatic opener and lock garage door.
❏ Do one last thorough search inside and out for anything that might have been missed.

1ˢᵗ week at your new home...
❏ Obtain a map of the area.
❏ Drive to the local hospital, fire, police and emergency centers to determine their locale.
❏ Take pictures of your new home.
❏ Contact your local Information Center; they may have baskets of goodies for you.
❏ Plan to have a second garage sale or find the nearest donation center. If you've moved items you find you no longer need.

_____
_____
_____
_____
_____
_____
_____
_____
_____

Top maintenance items that can be addressed at little to no cost...
(That almost always show up on inspection reports.)

- Clean gutters inside and out!

- Check all windows and doors to ensure they open and close properly. Also check the latching mechanisms to be sure they operate properly. Insulate, lubricate and repair as needed.

- Caulk all joints and seams that are exposed.

- Re-point bricks.

- Adjust garage door opener safety setting to assure it opens and closes doors properly.

- Trim bushes and trees and/or clear away from house.

- Be sure ground covers are low and not touching the home's siding.

- Lay plastic in crawl space for moisture control and remove ALL loose debris from crawl space.

- Check all outlets and outlet plates for proper function. Consider purchasing an inexpensive tester.

- Replace all non-working light bulbs.

- Replace/repair rotted wood.

- Install new furnace filters.

- Check all plumbing fixtures for leaks/drips and repair or replace as necessary.

- Check proper function of oven, stove and dishwasher. Repair/clean as necessary.

- Check all smoke alarms and carbon monoxide detectors. Unless recently done, replace all the batteries.

Add your items:

_____

_____

_____

_____

_____

_____

_____

_____

_____

_____

_____

_____

_____

_____

_____

_____

_____

_____

_____

_____

_____

_____

Seller listing paperwork checklist

Your firm may very well have a listing checklist but here is one to help you get started.

- Exclusive Right to Sell Listing Agreement
- Working with Real Estate Agent Brochure
- Sample Offer to Purchase and Contract
- Sample Professional Services Disclosure
- Short sale? Include listing Short Sale Addendum.
- CMA documentation, including all supporting material
- MLS entry review sheet (May be available through your MLS or firm.)
- Lead Based Paint Disclosure (if applicable)
- Residential Property Disclosure Form
- Be sure to store all correspondence and documentation associated with all transactions a minimum of three years per NC Real Estate Commission rules. (check your firm's policies and procedures)

_____

_____

_____

_____

_____

_____

_____

_____

_____

_____

Document, Document and Document!

Buyer paperwork checklist

Your firm may very well have a buyer's checklist but here is one to help you get started.

- Buyer Representation Agreement
- Working with Real Estate Agents Brochure
- Sample Offer to Purchase and Contract plus all appropriate Addenda (not required but a good idea and a great way to use an assumptive statement such *as "Now Mr. and Mrs. Buyer, I'd like you to review this sample OTP&C so when we fill one out you'll already be familiar with it."*)
- Copy of the Professional Services Disclosure Form (same assumptive statement as above)
- Copies of pertinent MLS sheets
- Loan information as provided by lender
- All correspondence and documentation is to be filed for a minimum of three years per NC Real Estate Commission rules. (Check your company's policies and procedures)

_____
_____
_____
_____
_____
_____
_____
_____
_____
_____
_____
_____

Document, Document and Document!!

Buyer/seller OTP&C paperwork checklist

Your firm may have an Offer to Purchase and Contract checklist but here is one to help you get started.

- Signed copies of OTP&C
- Signed copies of all addenda
- CMA documentation (if applicable)
- HUD-1
- Loan information as provided by lender
- Professional Services Disclosure Agreement (if applicable)
- Lead Based Paint Disclosure (if applicable)
- Residential Property Disclosure Form
- All correspondence that contains any decisions related to the transaction.
- All unique paperwork associated with each specific transaction, including but not limited to inspections:

  - WDIR (Wood Destroying Insect Report)
  - Mechanical/structural
  - Radon
  - Lead
  - Soil absorption test (aka *perc* test, short for percolation test. To add to the confusion, *perc* is often spelled *perk*.)
  - Electrical
  - Flood
  - Structural

Your list:

_____

_____

_____

_____

Document, Document and Document!

About the author

Terry Wilson was born and raised in Vestal, NY. He moved to Charlotte, NC in 1979. A graduate of UNC Charlotte, he joined IBM in 1981 where he discovered his true passion for teaching. In 1994 he joined a local personal computer training company and traveled the southeast teaching students the new world of Windows and the accompanying Microsoft products. Married and with a young son he wanted to spend more time at home and real estate seemed to be the answer. He successfully ventured into investment properties but soon turned to assisting others with buying and selling real estate. Over time, the teaching bug bit once again and so he returned to the classroom. He currently teaches pre-licensing and post-licensing courses and Continuing Education for Superior School of Real Estate and is the author of two Continuing Education courses; "Get into your Zone: a guide to zoning" and "Smooth Closings: from listing to contract, steps to take for a smooth closing". He also wrote and narrated "Hiking the Real Estate Trail: A guide to obtaining your license" a popular audio CD book that provides licensure examination instruction and guidance to pre-licensing students.

He holds the following designations: Certified Residential Specialist (CRS), Senior Real Estate Specialist (SRES), Graduate of Realtor Institute (GRI) and Distinguished Real Estate Instructor (DREI), a designation he is most proud of and one that is held by fewer than one hundred and twenty real estate instructors nationwide.

Terry is also Broker/Owner of Wilson Realty, a growing real estate firm located in the Lake Norman area in Mecklenburg County.

You can contact him at: Terry@WilsonRealtync.com

Trail log notes

Made in the USA
Charleston, SC
19 June 2014